THE ART OF SELF-RENEWAL

To J.H.M. and H.M.M.

THE

Art of Self-Renewal

BALANCING PRESSURE
AND PRODUCTIVITY
ON AND OFF THE JOB

Dr. Barbara Mackoff

LOWELL HOUSE
Los Angeles

CONTEMPORARY BOOKS
Chicago

Library of Congress Cataloging-in-Publication Data

Mackoff, Barbara.
  The art of self-renewal: balancing pressure and productivity on and off the job /
Barbara Mackoff.
     p. cm.
  Includes bibliographical references.
  ISBN 0-929923-80-4
  1. Job stress. 2. Leisure. 3. Labor productivity. 4. Family and work. 5. White col-
lar workers—Time management. I. Title.
  HF5548.85.M23 1992
  650.1—dc20   91-35943
                                                       CIP

Requests for such permissions should be addressed to:
Lowell House
2029 Century Park East, Suite 3290
Los Angeles, CA 90067

Publisher: Jack Artenstein
Vice-President/Editor-in-Chief: Janice Gallagher
Director of Marketing: Elizabeth Duell Wood
Design: Nancy Freeborn

Manufactured in the United States of America
10 9 8 7 6 5 4 3 2 1

Portions of this book previously appeared in *Leaving the Office Behind.*

CONTENTS

ACKNOWLEDGMENTS

Special thanks to Janice Gallagher for her wonderfully pointed questions; Darlene Cox for her generous and professional partnership in preparing the manuscript; and to Jeremy and Hannah: to see you is to be renewed.

THE ART OF SELF-RENEWAL

Why Balance Is Good for Business

At a cypress-green resort in Florida—where the country's top information executives were golfing and conferencing—one working wife lowered her husband's handicap with this tale: "Last summer, Jeffrey was working seven days and seven nights in a row until I insisted that he take the next weekend off. I warned him that if he came home with his briefcase on Friday, I would toss it in the pool. On Friday night, when he arrived with his briefcase, I grabbed it at the door and tossed it into the pool. *On that day, I found out that my husband could walk on water!*"

"Walk on water." What an accurate job description for most of us in this era of ferocious competition, smaller budgets, reduced head counts, smarter customers, and shorter development and delivery times. Those of you who survived the trimming and reshaping of the corporate landscape are faced with both an unprecedented workload and an uncertain future. Your marching orders: do more with less and do still more tomorrow.

WORKAHOLIC
OR WORK-HAUNTED?

Yet as we move closer to the millennium, the term *workaholic* has lost its meaning for two radically different reasons. First, as former Arco manager and writer Robert McGarvey explains, "Everybody used to know who was a workaholic—she was the woman with the same job as yours, working 25 extra hours a week. But now, *everybody* works that hard."

Welcome to the era of the work-haunted, where staff and managers are haunted by demands, and job security is a nostalgic notion; where even working around the clock won't get the job done or ensure that the job will be there tomorrow; and where job stress gets more press than Madonna. For example, in a recent study published by Northwest National Life Insurance, 7 of 10 workers said that excess stress was cutting into their productivity.

Another reason for the retirement of workaholics appears with increasing frequency in books and op-ed pages, on television, and in film, where we encounter stories of the formerly career-driven, haunted by past excesses, who have awakened to smell the decaf. Consider Amy Salzman's book, *Downshifting*, packed with portraits of self-absorbed careerists of all ages fleeing the fast track, or John Robinson's study, conducted at the University of Maryland's "Use of Time Project," in which 77 percent of the 1,001 people polled said that spending time with family and friends was a top priority.

Rewind your VCR and watch the last supper of TV's ongoing professional potluck, "thirtysomething," in which ad executive Michael Steadman quit his high-paying but soul-crushing job. And look at filmmaker Mike Nichols, whose last film, *Working Girl*, was an ode to ambition but whose latest film, *Regarding Henry*, features a driven attorney whose head injury helps him find his humanity.

Welcome to the era of the work-haunted, where we find ourselves pursuing both the impossible demands of work *and* the desire for a richer life outside the office; where the conversation at the next table is about job security and personal serenity, making money, and making meaning; where professionals surprise themselves by talking about "balance"—an idea they packed away in mothballs along with hyphenated names, "having it all," and "quality time."

This wave of interest in balancing personal and professional time presents a fascinating challenge to the work-haunted. With tight-fisted times ahead, it is clear that the ability to respond to increased job demands—yet keep pressure from undermining performance—will be *the* key to productivity and success. But at the same time, professionals and managers appear driven in what seems to be the opposite direction—to seek a balance between the pressure of the job and the pleasure of a rich private life.

How can we reconcile such opposing needs? Is it possible to recapture your personal life without compromising your career? Shall the twain never meet?

Enter the art of self-renewal.

RENEWAL: A PARADOX OF PRODUCTIVITY

For the last decade, my work as a management psychologist has provided me a front-row seat to understand how pressure undermines productivity on the job. I have watched clients invest thousands of dollars in productivity training without questioning the other side of the equation: What happens when employees go home from work?

Yet in almost every consultation with a CEO or training session I conduct someone wonders, "I can handle the pressure of the job, but how do I keep from bringing it home?" Or "I hardly have any free time; how can I recharge my batteries so I can bring more energy back to my job?"

During those years, I often met with the partners of these harried professionals. Sitting at annual meetings and corporate black-tie ceremonies, I heard every possible variation of the old joke: "My husband/wife is always working; do you have any perfume/cologne that smells like a desk?" But as I listened, I became convinced that life at home was not funny or fun. Rather than being an oasis away from the office, home had become another arena for pressure.

To start with statistics, 60 percent of American families are two-job couples, so not only are there fewer people to do the work in the office, there are fewer people to keep house. And once home, the lines between job and home are blurred by personal computers and fax machines in the den, the hours spent rehashing the office, and the briefcases brought to bed.

I began to understand the enormous risk, to both private and professional life, of unloading daily job pressures on family and friends. Of course, loved ones would be the first to suffer; how quickly we use up their empathy and concern in our preoccupation with performance. But when we foul the nest with work concerns, we extend job stress into an even larger territory of our lives. We risk being overwhelmed by pressure at work and at home with no relief. In the end, job performance suffers too.

So here is the paradox. You work long and hard all week, yet it is in the hours after work (with family and friends, at the opera or ball game) where you find the refreshment and rejuvenation that ensures excellent job performance. Where else but in the hours after work can you renew yourself so that you can bring energy and fresh ideas to tackle the unfinished business on your desk?

As I began to write about this paradox of productivity, I tried it out on the president of a real estate development firm. "Leisure is the source of creativity," he said, in full agreement. I tested it with another client, a senior banking executive. "I'd love to read the book you are writing—just don't show it to any of my staff," he said, smiling through his resistance.

FOUR REASONS
TO RESIST RENEWAL

And what about you? I know you recognize the job pressures that haunt you after work. You are in the middle of a family dinner and you can't stop thinking about Thursday's meeting. You ask a question about your son's girlfriend that shows you weren't listening. You are sitting in a movie theater and you can't concentrate because you are rehearsing a presentation to a client.

You camped out in your study last night, falling into bed at midnight, but you couldn't sleep; you kept going over your agenda for tomorrow. When you finally fell asleep, you were awakened by a nightmare—the one in which your notes for a presentation to the board of directors are written in a language you don't speak.

Next morning you woke up irritable and unfocused, dreading your return to work. Worse still, your family wouldn't pass the oat bran; they were giving you the silent treatment. So you explained to them why you don't have time to barbecue: "It's tax season, I have a new product release, I'm short-handed, I have a piranha for a new client," you said.

I understand how you might believe that renewal is just wishful thinking, a luxury you can't afford. But pour yourself another cup of coffee and turn the phone over to voice-mail; I'd like to tamper with your beliefs for a moment. I'm convinced that self-renewal is both a personal and a professional tool—one that allows you to manage the pressures of performing your job by experiencing the pleasures of life at home.

Let's start with your reasons for resisting renewal.

Reason 1: "I Gave at the Office."

Dan Hesse, President and CEO of AT&T's Network Systems International, got married on a Saturday and was back in the office on Monday. Hesse is quick to add, "But we immediately began planning a honeymoon trip to Australia." How wise he was to invest in renewal and avoid the trap of giving at the office.

At work you give and give and give, not just money to charitable organizations, but your time and your very best behavior. Have you ever noticed how charming, patient, and attentive you are with colleagues and clients and how careless and short-fused you are with family and friends? Have you read the study about working men and women who were more polite to and interested in strangers than they were with members of their own families?

"But my family understands," you explain. "They know I am understaffed and overworked. Besides, they know they come first." And how would they know? By the way you hide behind the newspaper or the way you bark at the dog?

"I have to impress people all day," you complain. "I don't want to have to try that hard at home." But you do need to impress loved ones with your care and interest in them. The son of a sales executive said it best when he overheard his mother on the phone with a client and asked, "Hey Mom, how come you never sound that nice when you are talking to us?"

"Giving at the office" is perilous in two ways. First, your loving relationship will starve on a diet of your self-absorption. Not only will you lose the pleasure of their company, but you will experience the corruption of your home as a castle. The more you give at work, the less you have to come home to, which becomes another reason for giving more at the office. As Gina P., the president of a publishing company, admitted: "Can you believe I'm still in the office at seven? I've got an angry daughter and husband at home and it's getting harder to go home."

In the chapters that follow you'll find ideas that will allow you to set your work aside, along with techniques for recharging your energy so you don't have to give it all away during the workday.

Reason 2: "This Is Only Temporary."

In the first quarter of his new job as executive vice president of operations at Adia Personnel Services, Jack Unroe declined to travel to an October sales presentation. As he explained, "I knew the road trip was important, but it fell on Halloween. I have a three-year-old son and in a couple of years Halloween won't mean anything to him; I just didn't want to miss it. I also wanted to send the message to my staff that family matters."

Unroe understood that a "temporary" tough time, like a new job, is not reason enough to postpone renewal in private life. He knew that the idea that a crunch is "only temporary" was pure myth. The detours on the road to renewal are endless: you lost a big account, collections are terrible, you have a project deadline. And so you promise family or friends: "I will be tense only until after the audit" or "after this big push, we'll take a vacation, we will make love, I'll help the kids with their homework."

This line of reasoning cuts two ways. To begin with, the crunch you call "temporary" will be followed by another and another and another, stretching out over a 25-year period; it's called a career. If you plan to live long enough to retire, you'll need to know about renewal. One manager joked, "I realized if I didn't stop calling everything a crisis, my tombstone would read: 'She's in an emergency meeting.'"

By the time you are available, your dear ones may not be. The damaging pattern of hurt and distance can persist long after the temporary tough time has ended. After a particularly punishing deadline, Valerie G., a magazine editor, admitted, "The crunch ended, but it's going to take a long time to repair the damage with my son and daughter."

As you continue reading, you will find tactics to help you reduce your tension about unfinished business and avoid bringing job pressure home.

Reason 3: "The More I Work, the More I Accomplish."

The Japanese have a word for it: *Karoshi*. It means death from overwork, and according to Hiroshi Kawahito, Secretary-General of the National Defense Council for *Karoshi* Victims, an estimated 10,000 workers a year die from it. Several years ago, while working with an unnamed division of Anheuser-Busch, I heard a disturbing variation of *Karoshi*. "It got to the point where almost every guy in this division had a coronary," confided one manager. "Everyone used to sit around—talking about how many hours they were working—comparing notes about double- and triple-bypass surgery. Having a heart attack became a Red Badge of Courage."

Extra hours are essential in the age of the work-haunted, but it pays to keep in mind the wonderful story of the saw (as told by Steven Covey in *The Seven Habits of Highly Effective People*). He writes about the man cutting a tree in the forest who looks exhausted; but when you suggest that he sharpen his dull saw, he tells you that he is "too busy sawing" to sharpen the saw.

The pressure to perform with precision over long hours, to make informed decisions, and to deal creatively in managing people and problems on paper are *renewable* job skills. And the only way to renew them is to take time off from work. In other words, those who don't take time off for self-renewal—to "sharpen the saw" with a vacation, a night at the movies, or a day at the beach—will eventually take time off in unproductive ways, through illness, accidents, costly errors, irritability with clients, and a lack of ideas.

Support for the art of self-renewal comes from both scientific and corporate headquarters. For example, British osteopath Dr. Donald Norfork reported on lab experiments showing that working too long on complex problems *increased* problem-solving time by 500 percent. Better still, just listen to the "pep talk" of the executive vice president of sales at Hewlett-Packard during an incentive session. "This is a marathon, not a sprint. We want you to run 50 miles, but why not run 10 and rest, run another 10 and rest? You can't run a marathon like a sprint and we want you to be working here in 10 years."

In later chapters, you will find workable solutions that demonstrate how the art of self-renewal can revitalize your job performance.

Reason 4: "Balance Is for People Who Aren't Serious About Their Work."

In the hard-working computer software subculture, this apocryphal story has circulated for years: Microsoft's billionaire president Bill Gates calls his staffers at home on Sundays to ask, "Why aren't you in the office?" Whether this tale is truth or fiction, we do know that the days of the cartoon executive who rewards his or her staff by saying "Great work, now take the afternoon off to read sales reports" have come to an end.

The emerging influence is that of the executive who recognizes balance as a tool of productivity. For example, at the Vice President's Roundtable, IBM Executive Vice President Jim Turner announced that he had unplugged his PC at home from the office mainframe—giving top performers his blessing to unplug from the office.

Even companies who work around the clock are starting to recognize that people can't maintain alertness, stamina, and creativity on the job without the self-renewal that comes from a rich life after work.

"Take time to relax," urges the president of a manufacturing company who sends his managers home if he finds them working too late. "I need you here *tomorrow*, not tonight," he explains.

The strategies in these pages can help you cultivate self-renewal as a tool to increase your productivity by learning to balance business and pleasure.

TWO REASONS
TO CONTINUE READING

If you are willing to table your resistance, continue reading. You will find two distinct reasons to practice the art of self-renewal. The first needs no explanation: You don't need to be sold on the delights of a Gershwin concert in the park, reading a mystery novel, teaching your daughter to do a somersault, dinner with a dear friend, lingering kisses, the first daffodils of spring, or chicken with 13 cloves of garlic.

But if even these simple pleasures have become a luxury, set aside to take care of business, then let me remind you of the second reason for renewal: *Balance is good for business.* Take, for example, the advice of John Fanning, former chairman of the board and president of Uniforce Temporary Personnel, who has been quoted as saying, "The weekend is a tremendous rejuvenator. When I arrive at the office on Monday morning, I am ready to kick down walls!"

SELF-RENEWAL: FROM THEORY
TO PRACTICE

Whether you pursue renewal to recapture the pleasures of private life or as a part of your professional portfolio, the book that follows will explore two avenues of renewal. We start with how to make a deliberate, and more graceful, transition from job to home, and turn next to the use of private time to relieve job pressure, renew energy, and restore perspective.

Beginning with the first chapter, we move from theory to practice. You will find dozens of techniques and tactics, examples, and anecdotes, drawn from my corporate practice as well as the wider (and wilder) worlds of literature, music, politics, and movies.

Don't expect to use all of the techniques with equal comfort and confidence. The idea is to consider a variety of approaches to the challenge of self-renewal. Your approach to transition and rejuvenation should be tailored to your unique personality, workplace, and relationships with family and friends.

Let's begin by talking about the transition you will make five times this week. You will leave work to come home.

PART ONE

The Job-to-Home Transition

1

How to Come Home from Work

When Dorothy clicked the heels of her ruby slippers in *The Wizard of Oz*, she made the most magical transition between work and home in the history of film. All she had to do to get from Oz to Kansas was to click those heels and murmur, "There's no place like home, there's no place like home." She awakened to find herself surrounded by Auntie Em and crew.

If we thought of Dorothy as a team manager, we'd have to admit that she had accomplished all of her objectives on that trip to the Emerald City: a heart for the tin man, a brain for the scarecrow, and courage for the lion. She had put in a good week's work.

Dorothy had no trouble leaving Oz. But for most of us, whether we have been off to see the wizard or to *be* the wizard, our transition from work is something less than magical. It will take much more than a click of our wing tips, or our power pumps, to ensure a smooth voyage.

You may truly believe that there is "no place like home." Yet you find yourself spending your time there distracted and self-absorbed. As one accountant put it: "I spend all day at work and all evening thinking about my work. And I'm not getting paid overtime!"

To understand the nature of the job-to-home transition, we can consult brain hemisphere research. As psychiatrist Pierre Mornell explains with great economy in his book, *Thank God It's Monday,* most of us spend our days in *left*-brain activities: using speech, thinking analytically and sequentially, verbalizing reasons and facts. To unwind, we must shift to *right*-brain mental functions, which are visual, nonverbal, and intuitive. "This explains why we are exhausted by words at the day's end, why we don't want to talk, why so many unwinding activities—like fishing, carpentry, and cooking—are visual right-brain activities," says Mornell. This shift is also the reason why the transition techniques that follow emphasize visual and nonverbal formats.

So coming home requires a kind of "homework": slowing your pace, postponing unfinished business, confronting your feelings about the day. This homework allows you to change your self-directed focus so you can encounter friends and family in a relaxed, responsive mood.

Here is the drill: To leave work behind and look *outside* yourself, you need to take one last look *inside.* This parting focus on yourself will allow you to cast off the pressures of the day and set the stage for self-renewal.

You can begin by shifting into a slower gear.

THE SLOWER LANE

Coming home involves the process of slowing down. Often the most difficult part of ending the day is shifting from the fast, demanding pace of work to more relaxed rhythms at home.

Denise R., a successful attorney, explained the problem. "I discovered I was applying the same discipline and organization at work and at home. Every *minute* of our weekend was planned and scheduled. I realized that I needed to stop applying the same intensity to every event in my life. I finally asked myself: What is the worst thing that could happen? The answer: We'd have cold cereal tomorrow."

The fast, intense pace that is habitual at work will block your transition to a relaxing time with family and friends. Here are several approaches that will help you to slow your pace on the way home from work.

TECHNIQUE:
Slowing Down

At 4:15 you may find yourself doing your most demanding work. When your day ends with a feverish finale, you will probably carry that intensity with you all the way home. Instead, why not schedule the least demanding tasks for your last hour in the office?

Diane G., a city planner, stays an extra half hour after work to unwind. She listens to soothing music on her Sony Walkman, writes in her journal, and consults her next day's schedule.

Plan to end your day with your easiest, least-pressured tasks. For example, try to use the last 30 minutes returning phone calls, reading professional literature, using the copy machine, proofreading letters, organizing your drawers, or cleaning the top of your desk. In this way, you are able to change the focus from your task-oriented day and become available for a refreshing and spontaneous evening. Yet, despite your best efforts, if you end the day talking 100 miles per hour with gusts up to 150, try taking a brief vacation.

TECHNIQUE:
Postcards from Tahiti

I once saw a picture frame that introduced me to a new technique for slowing down. The edge of the frame was painted with palm trees, blue sky, and a sandy beach. The inside of the frame was empty, except for the words "Picture Yourself Here."

Use your imagination to paint yourself inside that frame. Close your eyes and change your surroundings. Take a round trip from your stuffy office to Tahiti.

This application of the visualization technique can be accomplished by sitting comfortably in your chair and closing your eyes. Pick a favorite spot to visit. You don't have to go to the beach if scaling Mount Washington is your idea of relaxation. Just select a spot where you can slow down. For example, one financial executive pictures himself on a mule traveling slowly to the bottom of the Grand Canyon.

Did you pick the beach? Close your eyes and begin by picturing yourself walking on the sand toward an expanse of shimmering water.

As you settle under a palm frond for the afternoon, take in the smells and the sounds of the ocean: the fresh salty breeze, the foamy bubbles washing ashore. Feel the sun warming your face and hands. You are yawning and stretching lazily, maybe drifting into a nap.

When you feel ready to leave this island retreat, picture yourself walking slowly away from the beach. Then open your eyes. You will notice that your tension has begun to evaporate.

Practice visiting your favorite vacation spot on your way home from work. Even if you can stay only five minutes, you will feel rested and refreshed by your brief vacation. In your relaxed state, you will be ready to say a formal goodbye to the office.

LEAVING THE OFFICE BEHIND

I worked with James B., an executive of a chemical company, who ended his day with an essential ceremony. As he explained, "Every day for 15 years, I'd mark the end of my day by looking at my appointment agenda for the next day, and then locking it in my upper right-hand drawer. Next, I would leave the office, backing out toward the door and pointing to the drawer, as if it were a puppy, saying, 'Stay, stay!'"

His delightful closing ceremony reminds us of the power in saying a formal goodbye to the office, of doing what sociologist Irving Goffman calls "changing situational frame." Trying these tactics when leaving work can be the hardest part of your job:

TECHNIQUE:
Closing Ceremonies

Create a single ceremony that you will perform every day. Turn off the lights, turn the phone over to the answering service, log off the computer, and ask colleagues about their plans for the evening. One physician and his assistant shared a ceremony: each night one would say to the other, "Go home; you're fired." Another manager imagined that when she locked her office door it turned into a 2,000-pound steel door, one she would be unable to push open until morning.

No matter how simple or silly, you'll be astonished at the power of pronouncing that your day is done. Next, it's time to make a list and check it twice.

TECHNIQUE:
Listing

As five o'clock draws near, you may be facing the next day with a vague sense of dread. If you feel overwhelmed by the tasks to be finished, try to dissolve the dread by translating your free-floating anxiety into specific goals.

List all the tasks you need to do the next day. Create categories appropriate to your job and list each task under the appropriate category. Then look at your list. Can any tasks be delegated? Can any be handled later in the week? Finally, assign a priority to each task and a preferred time of day to tackle it.

TECHNIQUE:
Briefcase Check

You've looked at your list and, I agree, you've got some work to take home tonight. Still, I invite you to weigh your briefcase before you leave, and ask a series of questions:

- What kind of work am I bringing home? (On a scale of 1 to 10, how urgent is it? Could it be postponed? Could it be delegated?)

- Am I taking home a volume of work that I can actually finish tonight? (Will I end up frustrated and exhausted because I didn't finish all of it?)

- What is the best use of my time tonight? (Could I use time off for rejuvenation—a movie, a ball game—or should I cuddle up to the budget projections?)

Once you have unburdened your briefcase, you can consider the work left behind.

POSTPONING
UNFINISHED BUSINESS

I have often wondered about Mozart at the end of a difficult day. Unable to resolve the horn section in his latest opus, he was, I'm sure, terrible company at dinner that evening. Yet coming home from work with an unfinished symphony on your mind is an experience I'm sure you recognize. Even though you've checked your briefcase, you still bring home something more than paperwork.

You probably feel pursued by the phone calls you didn't make or return. Maybe you are working under a deadline. Your boss wants to see you tomorrow afternoon and you don't know why. You need a new idea to present to a client next week and your mind is completely blank.

Now consider this simple fact: some unfinished business cannot be finished at home. Why deny yourself an evening of rest and recuperation? Instead of "working overtime," accomplishing nothing, why not dance on your kitchen floor, explain an isosceles triangle to your daughter, and return to work the next day feeling refreshed?

If you really plan to come home from work, you need to find ways to postpone the completion of your own unfinished symphonies. My dear friend, analyst Leonard Mandel, used to call this "postponing anxiety." You can do this with three techniques that allow you to leave your unfinished business on your desk.

TECHNIQUE:
Seeing and Believing

Mentally review your agenda list. After you read each item, close your eyes and imagine yourself finishing that task.

Your list may include making a sales presentation to a client or tackling a mound of paperwork. See yourself shaking hands with an interested client after your presentation; picture yourself reaching the bottom of your in-basket.

Consider every item on the list. Visualize the best possible outcome: you were awarded the contract, you completed the report, and your staff followed all of your instructions.

You can end your day with a picture of yourself completing tomorrow's work. This kind of relief from unfinished business can be a powerful tool in your successful passage from work to home.

But some of the items on your list are problems that require a creative solution. You may not be able to picture the solution and this keeps the problem on your mind. If this is the case, try the next technique.

TECHNIQUE:
Delegate to Your Unconscious Mind

You may think that problems at work can be solved only with the focused attention of your conscious mind. When you are pursued by a problem at work, you will have difficulty enjoying your hours at home. Your mind will drift back to the problem you left on your desk; your family will find you aloof and preoccupied.

Think for a moment. How many times have you left a thorny problem with the intention of "sleeping on it," only to wake up with a solution? The next time you feel fresh out of ideas, why not delegate the assignment to your unconscious mind?

To employ this technique, remind yourself that you have spent several days or hours of deliberate thought about the problem and that you don't have any new solutions. Then, decide to delegate: "As I relax this evening and sleep tonight, I am going to turn this problem over to my unconscious resources. In the morning (or by 4 o'clock tomorrow) I can expect some fresh ideas on the subject."

This technique can work only if you believe in the power of these resources. Expect to get wild hunches while showering, new ideas while you are jogging, and creative solutions while you are brushing your teeth, and you will.

If these techniques fail, and you are still brooding about unfinished business, take a lesson from Lady Macbeth.

TECHNIQUE:
"Thought Stopping"

In the last act of Shakespeare's *Macbeth,* we learn that Lady Macbeth still hasn't recovered from working the night shift. We find her sleep-walking, going through the motions of washing her hands. She mutters, "Out, damned spot!" as she attempts to cleanse her thoughts of the night's bloody work.

I hope that your daily tasks are considerably less haunting than murdering a royal relative. But still, you can see that this distressed lady was trying, without success, to use a technique that you can learn right now.

It is called *thought stopping* and that famous phrase, "Out, damned spot!" is the perfect command to interrupt the thoughts about work that you can't wash out of your mind.

Consider Steven B.'s situation. His job in strategic planning involved giving monthly reports to the senior management team in a large organization. For days before his presentation, Steven would be haunted with doubts: Will I stammer? Have I picked the best slides? What if they don't laugh at my opening joke? Afterward, Steven would engage in a detailed review of his performance.

When you are preoccupied with similar fears, try saying loudly "Stop!" This command interrupts your negative review of the day or preview of the future and offers the opportunity to redirect your thinking.

If, like Steven, you are worried about choosing the perfect opening line for your report, try substituting a more positive scenario. Interrupt the flow of negative thoughts by imagining a group of smiling faces around the conference table.

With practice, you can postpone your unfinished business and enjoy your evenings at home. That is, if you can forget about the people you have encountered during the day.

UNWELCOME GUESTS

Guess who's coming to dinner? Your most sarcastic colleague, your pompous boss, and all of your clients who have recently undergone charisma-bypass surgery. You say you don't like the guest list? Just think how many times you have brought these people home with you, taking all of dinner and into dessert to describe their antics. You may as well have set extra places for them.

The transition from job to home requires that we leave uninvited guests behind—a tall order, as work is a contact sport and each day can bring encounters with difficult or disturbing people.

The difficult people will vary with your job description. If your job has a strong element of public contact, you may encounter angry people and unpredictable clients, students, and customers. If you are a manager, you may be plagued with uncooperative employees or unsympathetic supervisors.

Many public sector employees and health practitioners work with people who touch them with a deep sense of sadness. One pediatric nurse I know had to change her assignment because she was spending her evenings in despair about the beautiful, terminally ill children in her section of the hospital.

Because of your intense encounters with people, you may be coming home with uninvited guests for dinner. Later we will focus on the process of talking to family and friends about work. But now, let's talk about how to create some distance from the close encounters of the day.

The easiest way to do this is to take one last look at your encounters before you walk through the front door. Each of the three techniques in this section creates an opportunity to take a quick last look at the people in your day and to make a connection with your feelings about these encounters.

Your day moved so swiftly that you may be unaware of the unexpressed feelings about the people you have been "bringing home to dinner." These difficult encounters and unspoken feelings may have left you in a funk that you can't explain. If you are unaware of your feelings, you will have difficulty leaving the day behind. Your family may spend the evening playing that unpopular parlor game, "What's wrong with Mom tonight?"

Each of the three techniques in this section assumes your responsibility in spending time to discover how your day has affected you. This is a vital aspect of coming home from work.

TECHNIQUE:
Roll the Credits

Borrow this technique from the movies. In most films, the cast of characters runs at the end of the movie. This signals the end of the movie and helps the audience review who danced and kissed and died during the preceding 90 minutes.

You can roll the credits and acknowledge the end of your day by reviewing the day's action. Try to recall different people who played a part in your day. Name the cast. Identify those who played a starring role because they took up so much of your time. Which bit players achieved star status because of your feelings about them?

Get a mental image of the people in your day. Give credit where credit is due. Then, use the next technique to make a connection with your feelings about these characters.

TECHNIQUE:
Connect the Feelings

If you can identify and connect with your feelings on the way home from work, you can prevent a disastrous evening. Why waste four hours slamming cupboards or hiding behind a magazine when you can identify your strongest feelings before you arrive home? Or, put another way, in an ancient Chinese proverb: "You cannot prevent the bird of sorrow from flying over your head, but you can prevent him from making a nest in your hair."

Here is how connecting with her feelings worked for Susan P., an information services manager who came home after she found out that her department budget had been cut in half. Susan's head was pounding, and she was overwhelmed by feelings of anger and disappointment. When her husband came whistling through the door she caught herself and said, "Listen, I had a horrible day, and I am inconsolable right now. Anything you say will make me angry or make me cry. I think I'll just stay in bed this evening."

The ending? Her husband, thus alerted, brought her a cool green salad and poached salmon—dinner in bed. Fairy tale? Try this technique and transform your evenings at home. Practice identifying and connecting your feelings with the people and events in your day. You can probably identify the people who stirred you; you may find it more difficult to identify the feelings you experienced in these encounters.

When you rolled the credits, you asked yourself about the people who achieved star status in your day. In this case, ask yourself, When I left work today, what were my strongest feelings about those people and events? Then, consider a number of words that might express your strongest feelings. Frustration, anger, and confusion are common negative feelings in the work arena. But maybe you felt relieved, enthusiastic, or optimistic.

Anthropologist Fred Erickson calls this process "learning the language of emotions." If your habit is to ignore and deny feelings, connecting with your feelings may be a new and unsettling experience. In time, you will become comfortable in recognizing your version of anger or disappointment. You will know when you are feeling cynical or overlooked.

Your connection with your feelings about the day is the foundation of any evening at home. When you can label these feelings, you can prevent the evening from being dominated by your unspoken reactions to the events of the day.

Now, how about a nice, hot bath?

TECHNIQUE:
Bathing with Nancy Reagan

While Ronald Reagan reigned as President, his wife, Nancy, had a special technique for coming home from work. I know you are thinking, "Nancy Reagan didn't work." Still, consider the days during which she spent 10 to 12 hours in continuous eye contact with her husband and we must agree that being an attentive political wife is a piece of work.

Mrs. President's technique involved hot baths. In an interview with "60 Minutes'" Mike Wallace, Nancy revealed her success in cleansing herself of the pressures of political life. But the First Lady was not referring to the soothing effect of the hot water on her stiff neck or aching feet or circulatory system.

For Nancy Reagan, the most important aspect of bathing involved the conversations she'd have during her bath. Alone in the tub, she would deliver her half of a conversation with one of her husband's political enemies.

She would attack, argue, and rebut every innuendo and every enemy on the Washington Beltway. One by one she would attack them, in the tub, in these imaginary conversations. After these dialogues, she felt cool and removed from the close encounters of the day. (After Reagan's presidency, one can imagine Nancy using this technique to tackle biographer Kitty Kelley.)

This technique can work for you. Once you have identified both the difficult people you have encountered and your feelings about them, you can draw your own version of Nancy's hot bath. The idea is to create a situation where you can express your strongest feelings. You have the opportunity to state any angry, witty, sarcastic, or uncharitable comments that come to your mind.

Bathing with Nancy Reagan may mean writing a quick and caustic memo that you never send. How about an imaginary conversation on the bus or train home? You can mutter with your office door closed or on the jogging trail. Maybe you can scream in the car (windows closed) on the freeway.

Your version of this technique will cleanse your system of the day's encounters. You will be free to make plans for the evening that do not include the people in the tub.

Coping with Fears and Cheers

All the techniques in this chapter have suggested that you focus on yourself as a first step in your transition from work to home. I think that this phase of coming home can be described as the reversal of a classic Bogart line: "Here's looking at *me*, kid."

Before you can look outside your day at work, you need to acknowledge your hopes and fears, your stresses and successes on the job. Use these techniques to confront your future and to congratulate yourself on the highlights of your day.

TECHNIQUE:
Picture the Worst

I talked to Stan M., a successful contractor who had a definite image of his worst fears about his future. "I picture myself with nothing to do, sitting on a park bench surrounded by birds and bread crumbs."

Sometimes we come home from work possessed by our fears of failure or impending catastrophe. We come home carrying the heavy burden of unspoken fears about the future.

Ask yourself, "What is the worst that could happen?" Imagine the most catastrophic outcome for your immediate or distant future. Picture the situation that might leave you "sitting in bread crumbs." For example, if you are planning to give a humorous speech on Tuesday, picture an audience of 200 people, with no one laughing. Cringe when you think of all of them with poker faces, not laughing at a single joke. Picture people yawning and looking at their watches.

Usually such an extreme fantasy will make you laugh. But, more important, it allows you to zero in on your exact concern. In this case, maybe you should have picked a safer topic for the Kiwanis Club?

When you recognize your worst unspoken fears, you tend to rob them of their power. This happens because you force yourself to see the exaggerations and distortions in your thoughts about the future.

Yet, on other occasions, your fears may be based on reality. Naming these fears can build a strong bridge to another person. Later we will talk about how to share feelings of failure with people who love you. For now, use this solitary technique as a means of recognizing the unspoken anxieties that can sabotage your evenings at home.

TECHNIQUE:
Congratulations and Orations

We have talked about the stress and work pressures that haunt your evenings at home. The list included unfinished business and encounters with difficult people. Yet for many of you, the celebration of the day's victories and the prospect of your glittering future may be the source of your self-absorption when you come home.

"When things go well for me at work, that's all I can think about," said one stockbroker. "I am on top of the world and I don't need anybody else!" "When my wife walks through the door some nights, I get the distinct impression she expects us to applaud," said one husband.

Remember that only your immediate colleagues can understand the brilliance of your latest strategy. Have you ever started to explain a marvelous maneuver to your loved ones only to watch their eyes glaze over?

Here is an alternative to spending your evenings consumed with fantasies of your brilliant career: Take a moment to congratulate yourself, to savor what is gratifying about your job. Consider how the hundreds of nagging details of your day translate into the larger success of your organization, customers, or clients. Let your imagination soar.

Imagine the most spectacular outcomes of your present career path. Let yourself recognize your unspoken hopes and dreams; no dream is too vain or unrealistic to be considered.

See yourself selling all of the paintings in your next show, heading the environmental commission, or signing that huge contract. Discover a cure for the common cold. Travel to Sweden to collect the Nobel Prize. Remind yourself to write that acceptance speech for the Malcolm Baldridge Award. Picture your name in lights. Let the marquee on 42nd Street light up with your name and feel your eyes widen with the brilliance of the lights. Smile your most photogenic smile. Then, turn off the lights and go home.

A DIFFERENT LIGHT

By 1859, English landscape painter J. M. W. Turner had begun to enjoy his reputation as an eccentric. After his work was mounted in a gallery, he would arrive with his paints and palette to retouch his paintings as he examined them in the different light of the gallery.

At first this story reads like another tale of a workaholic; on second look, it provides a guiding image for the idea of using deliberate techniques to see your work in a different light. You have had the opportunity to catalog your thoughts and feelings about the day. As you get closer to home, you can take the next step and transform your feelings about work by placing them in a different, more humorous light.

Try the next two tactics to review your day by adding a comic touch. As you begin to see the lighter side of your day, you clear the path for others to move closer. When you laugh at your mistakes and pressures, you create the prospect of a refreshing evening at home.

TECHNIQUE:
The Sound of Music

The easiest way to lighten your thoughts about work is to add an imaginary musical soundtrack to accompany your recollections of the day.

Review the tense moments of the day and think of them as a scene from a movie in need of a musical score.

- Someone goes over your head to overrule a decision you made. (Frank Sinatra singing "I Did It My Way")

- A disc, an important client file, your notes on the budget mysteriously disappeared. (First four notes from the theme of the "Twilight Zone")

- You are asked to make coffee. (Aretha Franklin singing "R-E-S-P-E-C-T")

TECHNIQUE:
Choose a Comic Muse

In the classic movie *Play It Again, Sam,* Woody Allen created a marvelous device for his leading man, whom he described as being "married and still unable to get a date on New Year's Eve." This dateless fellow idolized Humphrey Bogart and was able to summon his presence for advice during awkward moments with women.

You can invoke a similar muse about the funny business in your day. In your case, you don't need Bogart. How about asking Bill Cosby, Robin Williams, or Lucille Ball to consider your day on the way home?

Picture yourself carpooling with a cigar-smoking Bill Cosby dressed in one of those expensive sweaters he wears in his forever syndicated sitcom. You are complaining about an obnoxious client and he is mugging in his Jello Pudding commercial style.

Why not invite Robin Williams to do a manic monologue about the quirks of your co-workers or envision yourself standing with Lucy and Ethel on the assembly line in the classic candy factory episode of "I Love Lucy"?

You don't need to imagine the exact lines or scenarios these comics would use; the idea is to enjoy the companionship of a comic muse as a means of helping you see your day in a more humorous, less stressful way.

If you still aren't convinced about the power of humor in easing your transition from work, how about considering the proposition that laughter is a terrific form of aerobic exercise?

AEROBIC LAUGHTER

When you laugh, your pulse rate doubles, your abdominal muscles contract, pressure builds in your lungs, your arteries expand and contract, and your endocrine system secretes hormones associated with wiry alertness. Laughter adds a new dimension to the idea of a workout. Did you know that the breath from a laughing person's mouth has been clocked at speeds up to 70 miles per hour?

According to William Fry, professor of psychiatry at Stanford University, "Laughing exercises muscle groups all over the body. It is an opportunity for all of us to exercise many times throughout the day. Many people laugh as often as 100 times each day. There is a difference in degree and intensity, but the exercise adds up over time."

If you are willing to participate in more conventional exercises, the next chapter explores some very good reasons for exercising as a part of your transition from job to home.

2

Running All the Way Home

"*I* just spent the entire day in a meeting; ask me if I am looking forward to working out," said the woman in the health club elevator, dressed in a silk suit and waffle-bottom running shoes. "I'm not," she continued, "but I sure am looking forward to how I'll feel *afterward*." Several haggard men—gym bags in one hand, briefcases in the other—laughed in agreement.

For many of you, running shoes, rather than "ruby slippers," would be the appropriate transitional shoe. You have found your exercise routine to be an energizing alternative to quaffing two martinis and slipping into a semicoma. I assume that the rest of you have a very good reason for not exercising.

Let's begin with your best intentions.

FOUR PERFECTLY GOOD REASONS TO EXERCISE AFTER WORK

1. Exercise Dissolves Tensions Accumulated During the Day.

Walter R., a social services director, described a tense encounter from his day.

> I have this co-director who has no control over his temper. Yesterday, at 4:30, he came into my office and accused me of making a decision without consulting him. He demanded to see copies of all of the letters I had sent out that week. His attack was so inappropriate and so aggressive, I had to concentrate all of my energy to keep from responding to him.

As Walter listened to his angry colleague, his sympathetic nervous system became aroused and ready to "do battle." At that moment, he was experiencing a series of physical changes including increased muscle tension, increased heart rate, rapid breathing, marked increase in the secretion of adrenalin, and an increased presence of oxygen, fat, and cholesterol in the blood. These physiologic changes are a response to stress that dates back millions of years. When our ancient ancestors were faced with a physically threatening situation, they could either fight for survival or run for shelter. This "fight or flight" response has persisted through millions of years of evolution and billions of stressful episodes at work and at home.

An associate's temper tantrum, an impending deadline, a misunderstanding with a client are all situations that can evoke anger, fear, or frustration. But the body doesn't distinguish between physical and emotional threats; whenever you are aroused or stressed, your body reacts with a primeval readiness to do battle.

Dr. James Skinner, professor of physical education at the University of Arizona and author of *Body Energy*, calls this predicament "emotion without motion." He explains: "You are tense and your body prepares you for action; but your job situation doesn't allow you to *do* anything! The tension stays with you and accumulates in your muscles. When you exercise," he concludes, "you burn off the accumulated tensions and your body returns to a relaxed state." This is the relaxed state that so many after-work exercisers report.

Walter R. confirms the experience and has incorporated running after work into his daily routine. "Running is my cocktail. It's my punching bag. It is the way I release all of my tensions from the day. When I run, I expend a lot of energy: I don't seem to be able to run hard and maintain my anger."

Carol K., a management consultant, feels the same way about her daily swim. "No matter how tense or angry I am when I get into the pool, I can't seem to hang onto those feelings, even if I try."

And Ted C., an architect, describes feeling like a "little puppy" following a vigorous Nautilus workout or a competitive squash game. "I have a vigorous workout, stopping short of self-abuse; I get into the whirlpool and I have gotten it out of my system."

Millions of runners, swimmers, tennis players, racquetball players, and aerobic dancers experience this kind of release from tension through their exercise.

Dr. James Paupst has written in *The Canadian Family Physician* about the symbolic aspect of resolving the "fight-or-flight" response through exercise. "All forms of exercise bring on the catharsis, even though it may be symbolic, of the stress reaction. The response fight may take place on the squash court; the flight may be simulated by jogging through your neighborhood."

2. Exercise Offers Time to Gain Perspective About Work.

Repetitive exercises like running, walking, swimming, and cycling allow you time to think about the events of your day at work. It can become a time to connect with your feelings about work and to gain perspective about the day.

Many exercisers report that as they begin to release the accumulated tensions of the day, exercise becomes a thoughtful, objective transition time. Architect Ted C. calls exercise "my only mechanism to detach. During the day, I build up a myopic viewpoint. After exercising, I can see where I was overreacting." (meditate) on the world

Walter R., who deals daily with an angry associate, likes to run with a friend and discuss the day. "As I continue running, I feel myself becoming less emotional, more rational. . . . It feels like a free-flowing catharsis." And two writers who swim report that ideas for work-in-progress seem to "bubble up" as they move through the water.

3. Exercise Creates a Diversion from Thoughts About Work.

For those exercisers who want to stop thinking about work, exercise is a definite change of subject. It immediately changes the situational frame.

If you participate in competitive sports like tennis, basketball, handball, and squash, you have to concentrate on your opponents, on your strategy for the game, or on signals from team members. The demands of these sports immediately divert your attention from work problems. "If I start thinking about the pile of papers on my desk, and I don't watch the ball, I'll lose," said one tennis player.

This shift in focus gives you "time out" from reliving and obsessing about your experiences at work. The exercise environment itself can provide a diversion. The colored leotards in your aerobic dance class, the sound of a basketball hitting the wooden court, the smell of chlorine in the swimming pool—each of these environments provides a sharp contrast to the sensory experiences of your work day.

If you exercise outdoors, your attention may shift to other stimuli: Donna, a physician, explains, "Being outside feels different and I experience myself in a different way: I listen to birds, I say hello to people, I pet dogs."

Intriguing evidence suggests that perhaps the time-out of exercise relates directly to your ability to return to work and tackle the problems at hand. A study conducted at Purdue University found that after a nine-month program of regular exercise, formerly sedentary men and women improved their ability in complex decision making by 70 percent. (Those who already exercised maintained their ability level over that same period.)

4. Exercise Provides an Opportunity for Private Time.

Although many exercisers enjoy the companionship of a basketball game or a running partner, others cherish exercise as precious time alone before facing a spouse or family at home. "I figured out that I come in contact with over 100 people a day," said Bert G., a cardiologist. "I used to enjoy playing squash, but now I find that I need to run by myself. I really need that time alone."

Dan Oliver, director of physical fitness for the Weyerhaeuser Corporation, tells a story about a manager who was approached by someone who worked for him while he was exercising in the company's physical fitness center. He told the employee, "This is my time. If you've got a question about business, I'll meet you in 30 minutes at my desk."

Karen P., an advertising copywriter, elaborated on this theme. "I do tasks and projects for other people all day. When I come to the gym, I change my clothes and take off my glasses; I get a fuzzy outlook as I go through my exercise routine. No one knows me here. I can be as self-centered as I please."

Despite all the good reasons, you still may not be exercising after work. You'll recognize these popular excuses and maybe you'll be willing to practice some techniques to refute them.

THREE COMMON BUT CONVINCING EXCUSES

1. "I Am Too Tired."

Cora R., a small-business owner, is familiar with this excuse. "I get to work at about 7:30 A.M., and by the time I get home, my choice is to exercise or to go to bed. It is always a big mistake to stop by the house to change. I see the bed, the darkened bedroom; the last thing in the world I want to do is to go to my exercise class!"

Like Cora, at the end of the day you may feel "too tired" to exercise. You assume that this means that you don't have the energy to exercise and that if you do, you'll need to be carried out of the gym on a stretcher.

But remember that many of the sensations you label as "being tired" are a part of the tension accumulated from your inability to act on the "fight-or-flight" phenomenon. Your body is housing a day's worth of unexpressed tensions. In addition, you may have been sitting still during much of the day and your body's systems are operating at a sluggish rate. When you exercise, you relieve accumulated tension and stimulate sluggish systems.

Dr. James Skinner explains that every form of exercise places demands on various parts of the body and the body responds to these demands, producing the sensation of stimulation and the energy you feel after exercise. Aerobic exercises, like swimming, jogging, cycling, jumping rope, and handball, have been found to produce the greatest stimulation of your cardiovascular system.

All of the evidence points to the fact that moderate exercise will make you feel more alert, *less* tired. The trick is to remember how energized you felt when you exercised yesterday.

TECHNIQUE:
Yesterday's Workout

The more you exercise, the more you can draw on positive memories to motivate yourself. The expectation of the benefits of exercise can help bridge the gap between fatigue and participation.

"I am always glad I came to class, *after* class," said one aerobic dancer. The technique, then, is to recall how you felt *after* the last time you exercised. Try to get a mental image of yourself after your run, or swim, or tennis game. Picture yourself after your shower, feeling relaxed and energized; see yourself bounding down the street, on your way home.

Remember, if you exercise after work you will avoid bringing guilt home with you. Marie-Anne J., a college administrator, confessed: "If I don't exercise, I just come home and plop down in front of the TV. If I do exercise, I might plop down anyway. But at least I don't feel guilty."

2. "I Can't Afford One of Those Expensive Health Clubs."

This excuse is reasonable enough. Those who belong to health clubs feel that the initial financial bite and the dues are worth the benefits of a regular location for exercise and the added bonuses of sauna, whirlpool, or steam room.

Money may be a reason why you can't take a sauna after work; but it is not a convincing reason for skipping exercise altogether. Note these examples of frugal fitness:

• For under $100, you can buy aerobic videos or tapes, a rebound trampoline, a jump rope, or a set of weights.

• Join a circle of friends to buy and trade exercise equipment.

• Organize a group of co-workers to chip in to hire an aerobics or yoga instructor for lunch hour or lobby for a company fitness program. (There are close to 500 fitness centers in companies across the country.) For tips, consult Dr. Kenneth Pelletier's book, *Healthy People in Unhealthy Places.*

And don't be a snob. The YMCA, YWCA, or local community center probably has a pool, weight room, handball court, and exercise class. Do you really need to be seen in the locker room of a fancy downtown athletic club?

3. "I Don't Have Time to Exercise After Work."

Time is a precious commodity after work. When you put family and domestic responsibilities on hold, it is difficult to justify exercise time. You may see exercise as an indulgence you can't afford. Or you may find that exercising after work will make your evenings too short.

But consider for a moment the idea that over a period, exercise takes less time than the family fights and sour evenings that result from coming home from work with unrelieved stress. You also might join the legion of early morning exercisers who say that exercising before work lends a different cast to the day ahead.

Exercise can't make up for lost time, but the quality of time that you spend with your family and friends may improve significantly. You may echo real estate broker Karen M.'s sentiments. "Driving home from work just isn't enough time to unwind. The day just sits there with me; I pack it in my briefcase. If I exercise, I get home later; but I walk out of the gym focused on what I am going *to* instead of what I have come from."

Even so, exercise can be a logistical impossibility. If this is the case, consider some other alternatives:

- Walk home. Consult *The Complete Book of Exercise Walking* by Gary Yanker.

- Park in a distant lot so you have a long walk after work. This option will entail slipping out of your Lois Lane pumps or stiff-backed wing tips.

- Jump rope 12 minutes on your living-room rug. Invest in a good jump rope like that from AMF Whitely Physical Fitness Products. Jump for 15 seconds, rest for 45 seconds.

- Exercise with a spouse, friend, or lover. Combine exercise time and social time. If you want to exercise at home, consult *Working Out Together* by Carol MacGregor.

- Exercise during lunch. Noon is the peak time for using the corporate gym. At noon, you can burn off the accumulated tensions of the morning, and exercising at any time of the day will increase your tolerance of stress.

- Involve your children in an exercise program. Dan Oliver, at the Weyerhaeuser Corporation, reports that spouses and children are encouraged to come to the exercise facility at noon and after work. If your time crunch involves children, have them meet you at the health club or community center. Or plan to exercise together when you get home, using exercise records or cassettes. Let each person exercise at his or her own pace.

- Involve the family in your sports league. Make your softball game a family outing, with dinner before or ice cream afterward.

- Try to eat a large lunch to cut down preparation time for elaborate dinners. Instead, spend the usual preparation time exercising and coming home to a snack or light dinner.

And speaking of dinner, any discussion about energizing transitions would be incomplete without mentioning food and drink.

NOURISH THE BEAST

Mavis O. is a record company's talent manager with a long commute home. "I sit on the freeway, half starved, for 25 minutes. By the time I get home, I am so hungry and cranky that I can barely say hello." A hungry person, like Mavis, will describe herself as feeling uncomfortable, nauseous, or irritable. Obviously, this is not the way to begin an enchanted evening.

"When your stomach is empty, its walls are being irritated by acidic juices," explains Dr. Brian Morgan at Columbia University's Institute of Nutrition. "Your stomach is contracting on itself."

Dr. Harvey Katzell, assistant professor of medicine at New York Hospital Cornell University Medical Center, believes that physical fatigue at the end of the day may be partly attributed to "coming down from a caffeine high created by multiple cups of coffee and scanty eating. At this point, the worst possible choice would be a diet cola that contains caffeine with no calories or nutrients. The cola will provide a temporary pickup that will deplete the glycogen in the liver and contribute to later feelings of fatigue and nausea."

Virtually anything a hungry person eats will reduce hunger pangs, but most nutrition experts, like University of Washington's Dr. Bonnie Worthington-Roberts, say that the problem with so-called junk foods is that they *do* satisfy hunger: "They supply calories without nutrients. If you eat a snack with these empty calories, you will lose your appetite for dinner and deprive yourself of needed nutrients."

An Apple a Day

Doctors Morgan, Worthington-Roberts, and Katzell all agreed that an apple would be an ideal snack on the way home from work. The apple received uniformly high marks for nutrients, fibrous matter, and quick absorption into the bloodstream. Other fruits, vegetable sticks, and cheese and crackers were also strong choices.

The message: Keep an apple on your dashboard or in your desk and stock your refrigerator with fruits and prepared vegetable sticks to immediately relieve hunger pangs.

HAPPY HOUR: CAN IT REALLY MAKE YOU HAPPY?

An editor confessed to a friend over lunch: "Things are getting really bad at the paper; I had to have two drinks before going home last night."

Happy hour, with its low-priced drinks and salty hors d'oeuvres, is a regular part of many working people's routines. Those who imbibe report increased feelings of relaxation and well-being.

The happiest part of the hour may have little to do with alcohol. You may enjoy the festive mood of a crowd where each person is trying to relax after work. You may unwind by talking about your day with the bartender or with your companions. Still, remember the facts about alcohol. Research regarding alcohol use has documented that after one or two drinks, alcohol affects the brain as a stimulant. Beyond that limit, alcohol acts as a depressant and you may begin to feel agitated, saddened, or frustrated rather than becalmed.

Changes in behavior may depend on how quickly alcohol is absorbed into your bloodstream. If you plan to continue drinking during happy hours, take these factors into account:

- Order a plate of apples and cheese. An empty stomach will increase the speed at which alcohol is absorbed into the bloodstream.

- Sip your Irish coffee slowly. Warm alcohol is absorbed more quickly than cold alcohol.

- Try to mix with water or fruit juice. Mixers like water and fruit juice slow the process of absorption; carbonated mixers, like colas and club soda, speed it up.

A handful of techniques from earlier chapters and 30 minutes on the tennis court may eventually replace the three-drink happy hour in your plans for the evening. The release of tensions and renewal of energy can help contribute to feelings of distance from your thoughts about the day. The more distance you feel from the day's work, the closer you are to home.

3

Turning In Your Suit

I was listening to my father-in-law, Dan, a retired CEO, talk to Ned, also a former executive. They were reminiscing about the cast of characters in the Fortune 500 Corporation they had managed in the 1970s.

"What about Mitchell?" Ned asked. "When did he *turn in his suit?*"

I smiled at Ned's use of this picturesque expression for retirement. Then I thought, "Most of us don't want to wait 40 years to turn in our suits; we want to 'retire' at the end of each working day." And most people, whether they work in a lab coat or a tweed jacket, change clothes immediately when they come home from work. They see the change as a first attempt to leave the day behind. "When I change my clothes," an attorney explained, "I feel like I am shedding the day, getting back to basics."

As you slip into something more comfortable, you begin the process of softening and transforming the professional image you project at work. "Turning in your suit" becomes the first homecoming ritual, symbolic of shedding the pressures and accumulated tensions of your day at work.

The theme of the vanishing suit bombards us in its endless media variations; we are amused by men and women who accomplish the transitions between work and home and love with just a rustle of silk or a whiff of perfume. I wish these transitions were as easy as changing your clothes.

Coming home from work in our cars and on buses and trains, we all struggle to unwind. We may be exhausted, preoccupied with unfinished projects and unpaid overhead, or elated and untouchable, absorbed in our success and career plans.

Those of you who spend your days presenting "killer ideas," "attacking new projects," and "knocking them dead" may recognize yourself in the myopic words of this project engineer. "When I am working on a really hot project, I think nothing of working 18 hours a day. Eating, sleeping, and sex are not important."

His words remind us of how self-involved we become in our jobs. In this chapter, you'll have the opportunity to sample homecoming rituals that will enable you to turn your attention away from yourself and your work and to become more receptive to your loved ones.

Let's begin with your world view.

AS THE WORLD SHRINKS

Have you noticed that most TV soap operas revolve around the details of people's lives at work? Hospitals and oil conglomerates are favorite settings. Once inside these workplaces, millions of enthralled viewers have witnessed the tiniest details of mergers, typing errors, and unnecessary surgery.

Focusing on the small world of the workplace is nothing new to most of you. As you travel home from work, you are preoccupied with the small, maddening details that soap opera writers adore. You can report every word of a peppery phone conversation, name each person who voted to reduce your program budget, and confirm rumors of office affairs — both the poignant and the expedient. In addition, you have probably spent your day focusing on a series of specific tasks. With your "nose to the grindstone," you may have assigned great importance to budgets, quotas, and forecasts.

The world tends to shrink as you focus on these people and events at work. Perspective is lost when you tie your sense of well-being to a small number of people and a small collection of details.

The next three techniques are designed to expand your shrinking world and to increase perspective about your day.

TECHNIQUE:
Headlining

Try the most obvious antidote for a shrinking world view; stop at the newsstand or turn on the news.

Pause at the newsstand and reread the headlines of the day. You may be surprised to learn that the story of the power struggle in your office is not front-page news. Linger for a moment, and think about how the headlined events affect other people.

Turn on National Public Radio as you drive and contemplate problems of an immense scale: world hunger, global warming, the plague of AIDS. Ask yourself, "What are the consequences, on a global scale, of my failure to land the Sears account?"

This approach allows you to hit yourself over the head with the obvious. It is permissible to think in clichés as you read the headlines: "My problems are really very small." "Life goes on without me." "Is my cup half empty or half full?"

Now, try the next technique and move from fact to fiction.

TECHNIQUE:
Science Fiction

Unexpected encounters with the future are a frequent theme in science fiction. Rod Serling and H. G. Wells have delighted us with characters who were catapulted into the future.

The future is *the* dimension that will change your feelings about today's work. The passage of 5 or 10 years will soften the impact of your present sense of catastrophe. But why wait 10 years? You can employ the technique of a science fiction writer to project yourself into the future and to create a healing distance from your day at work. You don't need to possess the literary gifts of H. G. Wells. Instead, substitute imagination and your knowledge of your workplace to create a fictional future. Kathleen S., a public relations consultant, begins her futuristic tale with a question: "In 1995, how important will it be that my slides jammed in the projector, and I had to reschedule my presentation?"

Continue to create your future. Picture your clients or your supervisor 10 years from now; see each person 10 years older and 10 pounds heavier. Who in your office is the most likely candidate for a toupee?

Which of your clients will be getting estimates for a face lift? The goal is to remember that as time passes, perspective changes. You don't need to wait to create distance from your feelings; you can envision the future on your way home from work.

If you prefer to reserve your literary efforts for the novel in your desk, try the next technique. Use space, rather than time, to create distance from your work.

TECHNIQUE:
Gaining Altitude

The court date was Wednesday and attorney Grant E. had memorized every word of his opening statement. He had rehearsed every possible question and anticipated all objections. He thought, "If I don't win this case, I'll have to spend another year as a junior associate!"

Each of you has experienced this pressure to perform. The pressure increases as you get closer to the demands and challenges of your job. Your stress level multiplies as you become strongly identified with the outcome of a particular task. At times, you may feel as if every decision and every problem on paper is written in capital letters. As you begin to examine your work too closely, you become cross-eyed.

Experience an imaginary plane ride to gain distance from your emotional investment in the people and projects at work. Book yourself on a fantasized flight that departs from a ramp connected to your desk. Settle into your chair, fasten your seat belt, and prepare for your departure.

Imagine your plane gaining altitude; look out your imaginary window and see your desk growing smaller below you. Within seconds, you will be unable to read any of the papers on your desk.

Watch the people become smaller and smaller; you can no longer see the expression on your supervisor's face. In fact, he is beginning to look like a tiny plastic marker on a game board. From this distance, the people and the projects look very small and you are far above the fray. Try to enjoy the view while you can.

With your new gains in perspective, you'll be ready to focus on the important people waiting for you at home.

CUTTING EINSTEIN'S STEAK

I once had a relationship with David, a scientist who tried to excuse his absorption in work by telling me a story that cannot possibly be true. He insisted that when Einstein sat down at the dinner table, he remained so preoccupied with the mysteries of the universe that his wife would have to cut his meat for him!

I refused to believe that Einstein's universe could be so small. But, apparently, David used this story to explain why he spent so many of *our* dinners sketching the design for his next experiment on my cocktail napkin. The message: If someone is doing important work, then everyone else must put their own needs aside and allow the great one to do his work.

Do you carry home this same kind of inflated idea of the importance of your work? Would you like to be working/living a kind of seamless existence interrupted only by meals and the sound of someone else cutting your food?

The problem develops because we spend the day at work absorbed in ourselves: our ideas, our decisions, our career opportunities. Work is the essence of self-absorption; in the act of concentration, we attempt to block out the thoughts and feelings of others so that we can focus on our own ideas.

One vital key to the transition between work and home is developing the capacity to shift from a concentration on work and yourself to a warm and responsive focus on the important people at home. The fantasy we all share is that once we are home, simply the *presence* of family and friends will allow us to leave the day behind. We also believe that if we really love someone, the transition will happen magically.

Jed D., a painter, explains his disillusionment: "I always thought that when I got married, I would easily leave my studio and the thoughts about my paintings behind. I thought this would happen spontaneously. Do I really have to make an *effort* to respond to her?" Don't assume that it is natural or "easy" to turn your thoughts away from work and focus on the people who care about you. Instead, make a genuine effort to become emotionally available at the end of the day.

Each of the approaches in this section is an opportunity to turn away from your own experiences at work and focus on your loving family and friends.

Let's start with your imagination.

TECHNIQUE:
Glimpsing

As you prepare to greet your family or friends, begin by creating a series of mental images that puts these important people in clear focus. For example, start with short glimpses of your wife's or husband's face. Fill in eyes, eyelashes, and eyebrows; outline his smile. Count her freckles and her wispy, occasional gray hairs. Take your imaginary finger and touch the tip of his nose. Try to hold the images as long as you can. If you have difficulty creating a mental picture, carry a family photo in your wallet or take a close look at the framed portrait on your desk.

Now, shift your thinking to recall leaving home earlier today. Were you both feeling angry about an unresolved argument? Did you linger at breakfast with warm, confiding conversation? Did you leave looking forward to a quiet evening or to a discussion of a visit to her parents? Change your focus and begin thinking about your partner's day. What plans did she have for the day? What frustrations or triumphs might he be bringing home? Picture them at home; what could they be feeling at this exact moment?

Take the time and picture each person you will greet at home. If you are on your way to meet a friend, use the same techniques to ease your approach.

Glimpsing provides your first connection with your loved ones at the end of the day. It can expand your capacity to focus outside your own experiences and become an empathic, responsive partner.

Now consider just one more thought before you walk through the front door.

TECHNIQUE:
The Thought That Counts

When you see someone carrying flowers at 5:15, you can be sure they have taken at least three minutes away from their own thoughts to focus on a gift for a special person.

When you stop to shop for a gift, you take a time-out from your myopic thoughts about work. You are forced to ask yourself, "What would he or she like?" You don't need to splurge. How about a photocopy of an article she would enjoy, a box of strawberries in the middle of winter, or madeleines on Bastille Day.

You won't arrive bearing gifts every day, so try window shopping as an active substitute. As a means of focusing on a friend or lover, ask yourself, "If I could bring Sam a present, what would it be?" Walk quickly past store windows and choose a shirt that would be just right with his new sport coat. Select a soft leather briefcase to replace her worn-out edition. Cruise a gourmet deli and consider bringing home the pumpkin tortellini.

As you select your real or imaginary gifts, you begin to connect with the affection and delight you want to express when you walk through the front door and greet your family. Before you walk over the threshold, let's pause for a moment to consider the person who may be waiting.

THE WELCOMING PARTY

Let's tackle the most persistent stereotype about coming home from work: the job-weary husband, greeted by a crying baby, barking dog, and harried wife. The stereotype is wrong on two counts: first, men are increasingly choosing to become home managers, and second, the reality of homecoming is one of worker meeting worker. Whether you have spent the day at home or in the office, you've put in a long day and there is a transition to be negotiated.

How can one partner get what he/she needs—quiet and a chance to unwind—while the other partner gets what he/she needs—affection, conversation, and a break from children, community, and kitchen?

If you are the partner at home, you can avoid what therapist Dawn Gruen calls "the arsenic hour" by preparing before your spouse gets home.

Leaving the Kitchen Behind

The preparation begins with deliberate acts of unwinding from your day's activities. Although some of your work will continue after your partner's homecoming, try to keep "working hours" during which you accomplish most of your objectives, so you will be free to enjoy each other's company.

Establish rituals of closure that acknowledge the end of the day. "At 5 o'clock, I put my feet up, read the mail, and order the kids to get dinner started," says one mother. Consider possibilities that will work for you.

- Employ a teenage babysitter for one hour in the late afternoon so that you can exercise, have a drink with a friend, sit in the park and read, or relish a moment of silence.

- Put the kids in a backpack/stroller/car and take a walk or drive that allows you to "come home" refreshed.

- Take a hot shower or bath (kids within earshot) and change clothes.

- Put on relaxing or rousing music—sounds of the ocean, Mozart, or Madonna—to change the pace or create a soothing buffer zone.

- Redirect your focus by reading the paper or listening to radio or television news.

- Kick off your shoes, pour a glass of wine, and congratulate yourself on a job well done.

As you participate in these rituals, use the time to distance yourself from the people or projects in your day. Remember that your unresolved feelings about your son's English teacher or an obnoxious fellow board member on United Way are just as likely to sabotage an evening as your partner's anger about a client.

TECHNIQUE:
Plan to Report

As you prepare dinner, shower, or walk around the block, summon the cast of characters from your day: Who was delightful or aggravating? Which community activities left you with a feeling of frustration or accomplishment? Identify three or four incidents that you'd like to share with your partner.

While thinking about today's most catastrophic events, view them as potential fodder for a situation comedy. Then ask yourself, "What's the funniest thing that happened to me today?"

If your partner is preoccupied with office business and you are concerned about your own unfinished work, you'll both be too self-absorbed to enjoy the evening together.

TECHNIQUE:
Gone with the Wind

Helen B. uses her son Charlie's nap time to do what she calls "focused work," including family finances and her work in the condominium association. Before her husband, David, arrives home from his law practice, she unwinds mentally by commanding herself, "Let go of those bills. I'll work on them during Charlie's nap tomorrow."

Helen's technique is a useful variation of Scarlett O'Hara's signature line, "I'll think about it tomorrow." But, unlike Scarlett, who expected Rhett Butler to take care of it, you can postpone thoughts and anxieties comfortably, knowing you will return to work tomorrow.

Now, let's meet your mate at the front door, where it is possible to ruin the entire evening just by saying "Hello."

GREETINGS: THE FIRST THREE MINUTES

Donna B. is a manager of corporate communications who found out today that her budget had been cut by 20 percent. She comes home exhausted, after spending the day scrambling to set priorities for her leaner budget.

6:01 Donna walks through the door, looking forward to an evening with Terry, but she is so tired she gives him a halfhearted hug.

6:02 Terry moves toward Donna, anticipating a kiss. As the recipient of an unenthusiastic hug, he feels rebuffed and slightly angry.

6:03 Terry berates Donna for not stopping at the cleaners. He starts reading the newspaper, treating Donna with indifference, and gives up his fantasy of making love later that evening.

6:04 Donna is confused and angry about Terry's aloof response. She tells him she needs to work in his study after dinner.

Obviously, both the marriage and the evening can be saved. But Donna had neglected to do the basic "homework" that has been outlined. If she had reviewed and explored her feelings about work, she would have been able to *separate* her feelings. Donna needed to separate her feelings on two fronts: (1) she was happy to see Terry and (2) she felt frustrated and exhausted from her day at work.

Mike P., a surgeon, summarized greeting on two fronts with wit and accuracy: "After a particularly horrible day, I'd say to her, 'Two things I want you to know: One is that I love you, and two is that if you come anywhere near me, I will knock your block off!'"

Warm greetings, when accompanied by hugs and kisses, can be expressed in 25 words or less.

"What a day! It's good to be home."

"I am ready to murder my secretary, but I'm glad to see you."

If you are the partner at home, be sure to avoid three phrases that are guaranteed to stop the evening cold, right at your front door.

THREE CHILLING COMMENTS

1. "Aren't You Glad to See Me?"

Many spouses perform a disappearing act when they arrive at home. Jean's husband slips into his study to play the piano or to use his computer. Barbara kisses Ron and grabs her jogging clothes to go for a run.

If you have been looking forward to a partner's homecoming, it is disappointing and hurtful when they seem to ignore you. You may wonder (and ask), "Aren't you glad to see me?" Paradoxically, it is in your best interest to leave your partner alone while he or she unwinds.

TECHNIQUE:
The Silent Partner

"I used to focus on him the minute he came home," admits Carol T., describing her engineer husband, Walter. "The kids and I used to follow him upstairs, sometimes yelling at him while he changed clothes. But I finally learned to let him change alone while the kids and I set the table downstairs."

Your partner's time alone is likely to lead to rewarding conversation later in the evening and to his or her understanding of your own need for quiet time. Try not to personalize your partner's need for solitude. Remind yourself that her or his needs are related to the process of unwinding and don't reflect feelings for you. Let him or her know about the importance of greeting you warmly and your willingness to be a silent partner for a time.

2. "Your Dinner Is Cold."

"One of the major differences between my first marriage and my second was when we had dinner," explained Jeffrey R., a psychologist with a home office. "My first wife had dinner hot and waiting the moment my last patient left. Without time to unwind, I couldn't enjoy the dinner or her company."

Although choosing a dinner hour cannot be considered grounds for an irreconcilable difference, the lesson is clear. Don't try to serve a nightly hot meal representing the seven major food groups. Consider the possibility that postponing or transforming the family dinner hour can reverse a collision course.

TECHNIQUE:
The Flexible Gourmet

- If you postpone dinner, prevent hunger irritability with simple snacks: apples and cheese, fresh vegetables, breadsticks wrapped in prosciutto or salami.

- Have dinner organized but not completed. Finish preparations while your partner relaxes.

- Cook together, or explore the possibility that he or she might unwind by preparing dinner.

- Prepare a number of entrees on a Sunday that can easily be reheated or combined with one another.

3. "Ward, I'm Worried About the Beaver."

You will be eager to share the progress and problems in your children's lives. But if you greet your mate with a blow-by-blow description of today's parent–teacher conference, you are likely to be ignored.

Washington parent educator Sylvia Hobbes reports that fathers' complaints about being "dumped with the kids" topped the list of frustrations about homecoming in her parent sessions. "I can't stand walking through the door and being treated like a babysitter," said one dad.

Once again, the key is postponement and a time to unwind. Let your partner greet the kids enthusiastically (see Holding Court, Chapter 10) and save your parenting conference for later. Too much talk about the kids can sabotage time at home; too little talk about each other and the world at large deprives you of an intimate connection with each other.

TECHNIQUE:
No Baby Talk

I recommend Hobbes's suggestion that each evening, either before or after dinner, spouses talk 15 to 20 minutes without mentioning the children. This change of subject may be awkward at first. Prepare by listening to the nightly news or reading a favorite magazine. Plan to relate a story from your day.

One couple took a step further and set an alarm for one hour so they could debrief together while their daughters played upstairs.

Cultivate the habit of deferring discussion of all domestic problems until you've both had a chance to unwind.

TECHNIQUE:
"About the Heating Bill . . ."

Sooner or later, you'll both be talking about the plumber, the dishwasher, and the VISA bill. Try later.

"I've learned to treat our homecoming as relationship time," reports Kate. "The last thing we need to do is to broach a task or be greeted with, "Did you call the phone company?" Raising these concerns in the first hours at home decreases the likelihood of resolving the problem. Establish a time (weekly or nightly) when you both can discuss problems at home.

You can survive your arrival with your greetings and postponement of discussion of the day's horrors. Then you can try one of two approaches to gain some delicious solitude.

TECHNIQUE:
"I Want to Be Alone."

The desire for time alone is why many people work late in their offices. After others go home, they find time for reflection and for a review of the day's events. The demand for time alone when you come home should be a delicate negotiation. In reality, it seldom works that way.

Ellen D., a purchasing manager, wryly reports: "My husband wants me to put a drink in his hand, give him his paper, put him in his lounger, blow his nose, and leave him alone!"

You are entitled to some quiet time when you come home from work. The question is how you communicate your need. You cannot simply announce that, like Garbo, you "want to be alone," and then disappear for a two-hour champagne bubble bath. Let your husband and children know that you are happy to see them. Then convince them that your time alone reflects your own needs and not your feelings about them.

Robin J., a local news personality, offers this approach: "When I come through the door, I put on a smock; and for 10 minutes my husband, the kids, and the dog can jump all over me. Then, I retire to my room to spend some time alone."

A mutual vow of silence can substitute for time alone.

TECHNIQUE:
Silence, Please

If you anticipate the need for silence, simply ask for it. Silence can prevent your evening from gathering negative momentum. Celia, an administrative assistant, told me, "Last week I had such a bad day that I kissed Steve and asked if we could maintain radio silence for the first hour."

You can develop a large repertoire of relaxing rituals for your silent or solo time. Each of these activities will ease your entry through the front door:

Try playing music, petting the cats, working on a crossword puzzle, snacking on cheese and crackers, reading the mail, starting a fire in the fireplace, watering plants, puttering in the garden, reading magazines or newspapers, watching the home team, taking a swim or a shower, retreating to a hot tub or sauna, listening to music, walking the dog, giving or getting a massage, playing electronic games, doing needlepoint or woodcraft, watching reruns of "Cheers," perusing store catalogs, or shopping by mail.

Practice techniques in this book or do something you read about in a frivolous magazine: put cucumbers, tea bags, or shredded potatoes on your face. Then, stretch out on your bed and take a 10-minute catnap.

A GLASS OF WINE

In Napa Valley, I have heard a marvelous phrase used to describe a wine with complex taste. Last summer, I was handed my fifteenth sample of Chardonnay with the introduction "This wine has a long finish." I hesitated for a moment, picturing farm workers striking for health care benefits. I tasted the wine and understood the expression immediately. The wine offered three distinct tastes in rapid succession: sweet, tart, mellow.

The techniques in the last three chapters have been designed to structure a transition—a "long finish" to your workday. If you have read and practiced the techniques, you should be enjoying a heightened awareness of your feelings about the day and a sense of relief.

Now, you are ready to answer a loaded question: "How was your day?"

PART TWO

The Secrets of Shoptalk

4

"How Was Your Day?"

I *sland,* Aldous Huxley's utopian spoof, chronicles the business trip of Will Faraday, a British journalist who has been sent to the Southeast Asian island of Pala to scout oil leases for his publisher. On this most unusual business trip, Will encounters a storm in the straits of Pala. His boat is smashed on the beach and he scrambles up the island cliffs. Unnerved by the sight of a snake, he falls, but survives.

The first island resident he meets is a 10-year-old girl who suggests that he use a popular island technique for altering his traumatic memories of the shipwreck. With crisp authority, she insists that he tell her the story of the storm, the destruction of the boat, and the snake at least 100 times. She is not satisfied until the memory loses its powerful effect on Will.

Huxley's island lore bears a resemblance to some of the techniques described in earlier chapters. The difference is that the techniques recommended here are meant to be practiced *alone.* You would not expect family and friends to listen to your raw, unprocessed feelings about the day, nor would you ask them to listen to the same story over and over.

As an alternative to Huxley's tongue-in-cheek technique, this chapter introduces the art of editing your thoughts and feelings about work *before* sharing them with family and friends. Editing is guided by the "share but spare" principle of communication. The wisdom of this editorial principle is reflected in a familiar teenage plea: *"Spare me the gory details!"* Tools for editing "the details" include timing, translating, accuracy, shading, and humor.

You may object and say, "But my wife [or friends] and I share everything." I am not talking about withholding feelings; I am questioning the wisdom of expecting others to sort out your feelings for you. It is essential that you do the "homework" in previous chapters. If you practiced these techniques, you will be able to label your own feelings and gain perspective about the day.

The feelings you share can be edited to make them easy to follow and, thus, can lead to an intimate exchange with family and friends. In addition, if you can talk about work in a concise, pointed way, you'll have more time for other playful and intriguing topics.

Before you practice editing, take care to select the right person for conversation.

TECHNIQUE:
Choosing a Confidant(e)

Talking to the bartender has become a cliché of homecoming cartoons. The bartender is someone who has no investment in what you say; he will not be hurt by your words, nor can he hurt you. He is an impartial observer.

If you don't talk to the bartender, who is the right person? For Denise M., a small-business owner, the right person is a colleague in the same field, but not the same office. David E., an insurance agent, confides in the one man he trusts in his division.

You may find comfort in talking to someone who, unlike your family, understands the unique peculiarities of your work situation and may even know some of the same people, but I would caution you to evaluate the risks of confiding your perspectives to someone in your workplace. We often hear the expression "my friend at work." Just as frequently, we hear a story about confidences betrayed by former friends on opposite sides of an issue. Donna's story is a case in point.

Donna was a faculty member who enjoyed a close friendship after work with Lynn, a member of the same department. Donna had confided her doubts about the priorities of the sociology department and her lack of confidence in the department chairman. That summer, following drastic budget cuts, Lynn lost her position and Donna remained with a part-time teaching role. During the jockeying for position that preceded the budget, Donna learned that Lynn had passed on Donna's confidential viewpoints in the hopes of making herself appear more loyal and more worthy of retaining her position.

Yet many business and professional people report strong and thriving friendships that began at work. I'm only suggesting you weigh the potential risks (betrayal, gossip) against the potential gains (confiding in someone who understands).

Use these guidelines in choosing a confidante:

- Ask yourself: What kind of response am I looking for? Do I want constructive criticism? Sympathy? Advice? Do I want to think out loud or to vent anger and frustration? It may be helpful to get some critical appraisal of a problem from a co-worker. But with strongly controversial feelings, you may decide to talk to a family member who has no stake in the specifics of your complaints. If you are looking for sympathy, there is no place like home.

- Remember that your feelings at the end of the day are often distorted; they are intense and transient feelings. It may be safer if you process your feelings alone, using techniques like Bathing with Nancy Reagan (Chapter 1) or Gaining Altitude (Chapter 3) before you share strong statements of feeling.

After a conversation, the other person will not see the transformation of your feelings; they will remember your feelings as you express them today. Be sure to keep your confidantes informed of any changes in your attitude.

You may also decide not to talk about work at all.

TECHNIQUE:
When Silence Is Golden

Before you launch into your report of the day's events, decide whether you actually want to relive your experiences all over again. Natalie, a social worker, states her preference: "By the time I get home, I have usually spent some time sorting out my feelings. If Bobby starts questioning me about work, I am forced to relive it all again."

You need to convey your preference for silence with warmth and clarity. Like your homecoming greeting, your preferences should be stated in terms of your needs. You don't want your desire for silence to be interpreted as secrecy, a lack of trust, or an unwillingness to express your feelings.

He: How was your day?   *She:* A real killer. I'd like to forget it completely.

She: How was your day?   *He:* Pretty hectic; I don't even want to *think* about it tonight.

But maybe you *do* want to talk about your day; you have strong feelings and opinions and you have decided to share them with a close friend or spouse. Rather than jumping in, try the next two techniques to preview your conversations about work.

"THOSE STORIES AT ELEVEN"

You are in the middle of a wonderful Joan Crawford movie; suddenly the face of your local newscaster appears and proclaims: "Flooding on the Columbia, troops sent to Bulgaria. Those stories at eleven." This preview informs you of the top stories of the day and lets you know what to expect when you tune in the news at 11 o'clock.

You can borrow the newscaster's technique by offering a condensed version of your day and foreshadowing your intentions for further conversation. Ralph P., a physician, explains the need for foreshadowing the top stories: "I want the other person to give me a general status report of their needs before launching into a disaster they want to discuss. I hate to arrive at another crisis *immediately*."

TECHNIQUE:
The Condensed Version

The question "How was your day?" is a lot like the question "How are you?" Most people expect to get an automatic response of "fine" to either question. Your best opening response to the question of your day is one that gives the questioner a *condensed* version of your answer and allows you to postpone the unexpurgated version for later in the conversation or later in the evening. Your initial response should be succinct. Pick a sentence or two that summarizes your basic feelings and states your intentions.

She: How was your day?	*He:*	It's a long story. I'd like to get your opinion later.
He: How was your day?	*She:*	Really disappointing. I'm going to need a little tea and sympathy.
She: How was your day?	*He:*	Fantastic! I want to tell you what my client said about my presentation.

When you clarify your intentions, you can combat the problem of mind reading.

TECHNIQUE:
Exchanging the Crystal Ball

At 6 o'clock, across the country, more minds are read than at all the psychic fairs in Marin County. Listen to Ray B. as he predicts his wife's feelings. "When Janet comes in, I can take one look at her face and know that she had had a horrible day. I take my cue from her and offer to cancel any plans we have."

Some couples, like Ray and Janet, have developed elaborate mind-reading rituals that begin with a kiss at the front door and last all the way into the bedroom five hours later.

In this case, Ray knew that Janet, a travel agent, was worried about meeting her sales quota at work. He didn't want to put more pressure on her by asking her to make love during the week. When they finally talked, Janet let Ray know that although she was under pressure at work, she was more worried about the fact that Ray seemed to have lost his sexual interest in her.

Mind reading is an inaccurate, time-consuming trick. Instead of predicting the future, you end up *creating* the future based on your own untested assumptions.

Janet could close off the possibility of mind reading by letting Ray know about her day and her wishes for the evening. She could exchange his crystal ball for some straightforward feelings and requests.

"I'm really beat; how would you feel about going to the movie tomorrow?" *or* "Today was the worst; I am looking forward to turning up the electric blanket and cuddling with you."

Don't make your initial feelings and intentions a topic of psychic research. Once you have clarified your intentions, you have opened the possibility of talking about your day in greater detail.

When you "officially" begin to talk about your day, you will want to practice the *art of editing.*

THE ART OF EDITING: "THE CUTTING-ROOM FLOOR"

All films and books are completed with the help of an editor, someone who makes decisions about including what is essential to the main idea, and leaving the rest "on the cutting-room floor."

In this section, I introduce five tools for editing the presentation of your day at work. We explore the principles of *timing, translation, accuracy, shading,* and *humor.*

If you have done the "homework" in previous chapters, you will have a strong sense of your feelings about the day, but the feelings may not be in a form that another person can understand. If you are accustomed to greeting your family and friends with raw, unedited feelings about your day, you may, at first, feel uncomfortable leaving some of that day on the cutting-room floor. You may feel you are withholding vital information.

When you practice the art of editing, you'll find that your family and friends become more attentive to your feelings about work. This may be the ultimate benefit of editing: it leads to companionable listening.

Editing Tool 1: Timing

I hope that you won't spend your whole evening, every evening, talking about work. Every couple and every friendship should determine the right time to talk about work and set reasonable time limits.

My friend Hallie and I used to meet often after work. As we drove out to dinner, we would try to do all of our complaining about work before we arrived at the restaurant. Then, we could relax over dinner and talk about love and movies and politics.

Before you launch into a long story about work, you'll want to practice two techniques that allow you to keep your eye on the clock.

TECHNIQUE:
The Right Time

Your descriptions of work should be preceded by a brief environmental impact study. You need to take the other person's situation into account. Is your mate in the middle-of executing a complicated curry recipe? Maybe you should save your story until preparations are complete. Do you want his undivided attention? Maybe you could wait until the kids go to bed.

Choosing the right time depends on your awareness of your feelings and an understanding of the impact your statements can have. Don't set yourself up by announcing your intention to resign the minute you see your wife. She may need time alone to relax or to understand her own feelings about the day. You don't have to guess about the right time; simply ask: "I've got some problems at work. When would be a good time to talk?"

Next, practice the art of editing a long story.

TECHNIQUE:
"To Make a Long Story Short . . ."

We used to have a joke in my family: whenever anyone said "To make a long story short," it really meant, "Stay tuned, this is a long story."

Walter G., an airline pilot, explained his reaction to his wife's excess verbiage. "After a while, I stopped listening to Jane talk about her experiences. I kept thinking: get to the point!" And from Jane: "I used to talk and talk to try to get Walter's attention. Now, I look him directly in the eye and tell him a shortened version of my day, and he really listens."

Here are three guidelines for shortening your stories and lengthening your evenings.

• Don't give an oral transcription of your conversations. Only court reporters are responsible for a word-by-word account of the events of their day. Don't frame your story with "and then he said" and "then I said." These blow-by-blow descriptions are tedious to follow.

- Summarize the main points of an important conversation. Use a critical quote only for emphasis. "So after chewing me out for 15 minutes, he says, 'We really think you have a great potential here.'"

- Don't build up to your main point by including irrelevant information. Begin with your conclusions or the main point rather than leading up to it with dozens of tiny details. Start by saying, "He did it again, he picked Ed to head up the campaign." Don't begin by telling how you got the news about Ed: "First Vince called both Ed and me into the office. I knew something was happening since we didn't have anything important scheduled. Ed walks in, looking pretty pleased with himself . . . . "

If you really do have a long story, negotiate directly for the time to tell it. Tell your husband, "I am really upset. Can we take about 30 minutes to talk about it?" And if you bypass the time limits, don't continue talking. Negotiate for more time: "It looks like we went over our limit. Can we talk five more minutes to wrap it up?"

As you continue to talk, you may discover that your story needs a translation.

Editing Tool 2: Translating

Every profession has its abbreviations, codes, and jargon. After eight hours of using work shorthand, you are likely to continue to use it at home. This "in-house slang" is the easiest material to edit out of your conversations about work.

Joan, a city planning manager, explained: "When I start using abbreviations from work, Chip gets that glassy-eyed look. Last week I started talking about SUP-DEV [supervisor development] and MFs [management forecasts] and I could tell that I had lost him completely."

You may decide to take the time to teach your family about some of the basic terminology in your field. If not, be prepared to translate your tasks and accomplishments in language that your loved ones can understand. Follow three guidelines for translation:

- Eliminate abbreviations that are unique to your job.

  Court Psychologist: I had to interview the social worker from CPS and the diagnostic summary was heartbreaking.

  Translation: I had to interview the social worker from Children's Protective Services and this family's history was a long, sad story.

- Eliminate expressions you learned in graduate school.

  Architect: The Land Use Department is requiring that we put the parking lot below grade. That will put our costs way over budget.

  Translation: The Land Use Department is requiring us to put the parking lot underground. That will cost our client $10,000 more.

- Eliminate informal jargon that only fellow professionals would understand.

  Sales Representative: I don't seem to have any problem with prospecting; I just can't seem to move them to closing.

  Translation: I don't have a problem finding possible buyers; I just can't seem to get enough of them to sign on the dotted line.

  Next, continue to edit your presentations with an eye to accuracy.

Editing Tool 3: Accuracy

Dennis T., a real estate broker, came to work to find that his secretary had called in sick. He had a stack of correspondence and contracts that needed to go out that day, so he canceled most of his appointments and typed them himself. He postponed all of his client meetings except for one lunch-hour meeting. At lunch, he accepted a $25,000 check as earnest money on a $500,000 house.

When Dennis came home, he offered his wife, Karen, the following version of his day:

> *I had the worst day! Evelyn called in sick and I had to do her typing myself. I was behind all day. I only had one client meeting and had to postpone the rest until later in the week. I don't know why they don't get temporary help; they never get temporary help. I don't know what I'll do if they don't get someone tomorrow; I just dread going in . . . .*

Notice any missing information? It would be inaccurate to say that Dennis had a smooth day; he wouldn't want to omit the inconveniences and pressure of doing his own clerical work. But his description was inaccurate without the inclusion of the promise of a fat commission.

Try editing your accounts for accuracy by using this technique.

TECHNIQUE:
When Accuracy Counts

As you think about summarizing your day, use the clichéd but useful formula of good/bad news. Ask yourself: "What is the worst thing that happened today? What is the best?" Be prepared to share both kinds of news.

Edit and delete words like *never* and *always*. These words have a strong effect on both the speaker and the listener. Things will sound worse than they are to you, and you may elicit more sympathy than you need from a listener. Beware of crying wolf.

Consider the duration of the problem. Is this a permanent change or is it something that just happened today? Be sure to include a statement about how long the problem will last. My favorite example of editing for accuracy comes from an attorney who called his wife after losing a costly litigation to collect fees from a client. "Did anything good happen today?" his wife asked. "*Not yet*," he answered, hopefully.

Now, let's explore an editing tool closely related to accuracy.

Editing Tool 4: Shading

A technique called "Mount Vesuvius" was once very popular in therapeutic circles. Each person would take 10 minutes to spew angry and frustrated feelings toward family, bosses, and co-workers. I think the name *Mount Vesuvius* was rather apt in describing this technique; remember that the entire civilization of Pompeii was buried under the path of Vesuvius' molten lava.

When you are angry or frustrated about work, you want to share your feelings with someone, but you don't want to overwhelm them with your expression. Unedited venting of the Mount Vesuvius variety is not a form of sharing; it is a display of self-indulgence. If you are alone (see Bathing with Nancy Reagan, Chapter 1), you can enjoy some unrestrained venting. When you are with someone you love, you need to edit your feelings by shading both the positive and the negative experiences in your day.

Practice *shading* as you think about expressing angry feelings or gloating about your accomplishments.

TECHNIQUE:
The Color Red

Jules Feiffer could have been thinking of shading when he said, "Artists can color the sky red because they know it is blue. Those of us who aren't artists *must color things the way they really are* or people might think that we are stupid."

When you are angry or irritated, you will be ready to color a "blue sky red." The tendency is to express your feelings in the strongest possible terms. Mick F., an engineer, was trying to get some information about advanced graduate study and ran into an uncooperative department secretary. He described himself as being "furious" after this encounter. He groused, "I wonder if she ever got her high school diploma?"

Stress researchers have impressed us with the importance of mental labels. Most research suggests that stress is not the event (like Mick's encounter with the secretary), but the *label* that is assigned to the event ("I'm furious"). In this way, Mick's descriptions of his feelings might have influenced the way he felt: Was Mick really *furious*? What would have happened if he had decided to label his feelings as being annoyed or simply angry?

Remember, there is someone listening to you and taking your feelings seriously. Try to save them unnecessary pain or concern for you. When you don't edit and shade, you may convince yourself and the listener that your situation is much worse than it is.

You are entitled to strong feelings about events at work, but choose words that shade your feelings accurately. For every strong feeling, you have a number of choices about how to express yourself. Try to avoid hyperbole and hysteria in your descriptions of work. For example, are you feeling "concerned" or "terrified"? "Disappointed" or "crushed"? "Embarrassed" or "humiliated"? "A little blue" or "really depressed"?

Remember that sometimes you need to shade your success stories as carefully as your horror stories.

TECHNIQUE:
The Shades of Success

You have every right to proclaim your accomplishments to dear friends and family. Any friend who isn't genuinely pleased with your good work should be dropped from your holiday shopping list.

Gloating about your success is another matter. Depending on the circumstances, you may decide to shade the presentation of your accomplishments. This is not like pretending to lose at tennis. You are not pretending that you didn't win; you are simply taking the other person's feelings into account.

Anna S., a successful banker, explains the difference: "Within five minutes of getting into the car, Peter has told me about his day. If I have had a really great day, and his day has been frustrating, I tell him about my triumph. *"I just don't crow!"*

If you are hiding the *facts* of your success from your partner, your relationship is in peril. It is not patronizing to withhold good news; your friends and lovers are not that fragile. Yet in many circumstances, you need to exercise self-control in your tall tales. Don't think of shading as losing at tennis; think of it as an act of kindness and consideration.

Neil gives an example: "I finally got promoted to supervisor and I was so high that I felt like I should advertise in the newspaper! It was hard *not* to gloat, since my friends were all in dead-end job situations and were feeling frustrated, though happy for me."

Few things are worse than a friend on a narcissistic binge. You have great fun seeing yourself in the brightest possible light (see Congratulations and Orations, Chapter 1), but the occasions when you can share that light should be altered by your sensitivity to the other person's situation.

Begin to share your good fortune with expressions like "I had some good news today," "Something terrific came my way," or "I have something wonderful to tell you." But be prepared to edit the details, when you learn of a friend's predicament. For example, you have just been promoted and you are having lunch with a friend who is concerned about being laid off. It would be patronizing to withhold your triumph, but you could postpone the details. You don't need to dwell on your generous dental benefits and the view of the mountains from your new office. Tell her the details after her own crisis has passed, when she can appreciate the view.

Finally, draw on your sense of humor to edit your day with a comic touch.

Editing Tool 5: Humor

You examined your sense of humor in Chapter 2 and explored the possibilities of viewing your day in a more humorous light. As you considered the lighter side of work, many of the "gory details" were left behind.

As a tool of editing, humor helps you to shape your telling of the day around comical interpretation of events. Although some events are truly devastating, and are not amenable to laughter, most daily pressures and mistakes can be reported with a humorous emphasis. You can be accurate in your description of the frustrations in your day; just let the other person know that in spite of what happened, you are inviting them to consider the incident with laughter.

Three quick techniques may help you include humor in your descriptions of work.

TECHNIQUE:
Introductions

Begin telling a work story with an introduction that promises laughter. Make sure that your nonverbal gestures match your words.

"The funniest thing happened to me today." (smiling, chuckling)

"You are going to *love* this story!" (direct eye contact, grinning)

"Our sales meeting was something out of Looney Tunes!" (smiling, eyebrows raised)

These introductions help you to create the expectation of laughter. When you begin a story with humor, your laughter can be contagious.

TECHNIQUE:
Share the Laughter

If you have accomplished the feat of changing stressful situations into comic memories, share your perspectives as you talk about your day. Let the other person see the struggle you experienced as you tried to see humor in your day.

> *At first, I felt really angry about Emma. She always stares out of the window when I try to explain problems to her. Then, I started thinking how much she looked like that old Lily Tomlin character, the obnoxious telephone operator "Ernestine." She even wears that cheap costume jewelry.*

You can also try to imitate the difficult people in your day.

TECHNIQUE:
Impersonations

If you decide to repeat a disturbing or irritating conversation from work, see if you can add some imitations of the other person. You don't have to be Rich Little to impersonate the gestures and language of clients and associates you work with every day.

Nonverbal gestures are the easiest to mock: Does she fiddle with a pencil behind her ear? Does he wrinkle his nose with disapproval or furrow his eyebrows in concentration? Perhaps the person has a regional accent or drawl that you can imitate. English and southern accents are easy to impersonate; so are New England Kennedy–style pronunciations.

You don't have to use an accent to repeat a colleague's frequent use of irritating figures of speech, like "up to speed" or "is that right?" or to imitate a client's shrill, high-pitched laughter.

Your impersonations can help you to edit out some of the negative feelings and to share a light moment with someone at home.

But if the five editing tools haven't stopped you from presenting your day in the harshest light, try some emergency editing.

EMERGENCY EDITING

At the end of an exhausting day, you may not reach for your editing tools on the first draw. Many evenings you will forget to edit and belatedly notice yourself off on a tangent. You suddenly find yourself in the middle of a long story sprinkled with jargon and overstated feelings and delivered in an intense, humorless tone.

Don't give up the evening as a lost cause. Catch yourself, apply the brakes, and put your words and deeds in reverse. Here is how your emergency application of the principle of accuracy sounds.

You are building up steam, using words like "always" and "never"; you are making a temporary situation sound interminable. You can stop yourself: "You know, I think I am making this sound worse than it is. I know that the rush will subside after Christmas."

Now, let's stop talking about work for a moment, and listen to Hamlet's soliloquy.

HAMLET'S PROBLEM

Hamlet's chosen communication tool was the soliloquy. Shakespeare provided him with the material to make timeless statements about his personal and professional life. Yet his articulate conversations with himself didn't translate into meaningful discussions with others.

There is something about a soliloquy, no matter how eloquent, that discourages conversation. "To be or not to be?" was a rhetorical question, one that most listeners in the audience wouldn't touch.

As you travel home, editing your thoughts about work, you are engaged in a soliloquy about your day. When you come home to an audience of family and friends, you'll want to change your format from a monologue to a *dialogue*. You can avoid Hamlet's problem and ask a series of questions to punctuate your soliloquies about work. You can break the silence and ask others to join you in a dialogue about your day.

TECHNIQUE:
"That Is the Question . . . ."

Follow these three guidelines to initiate dialogue:

- Note the other person's nonverbal cues. If the listener's eyes become glassy or vacant, ask "Am I going on too long?" If someone looks confused, ask "Did I leave something out?" or "You look confused, are you still with me?"

- If you want advice, ask for it directly. Don't expect the other person to know why you are telling a story. Be explicit about your intentions. You can say, "So what do you think he's up to?" or "How would you handle this?" or "What do you think; do you think I blew it?"

- Use questions to punctuate your stories. Tell the listener that he will appreciate the story because it will remind him of another person or situation. "Doesn't this sound like the stunt Alex used to pull? How did you ever get him under control?"

You are entitled to as much air time as you have negotiated. But if you want to move beyond Hamlet's style, you need to ask questions that stimulate dialogue and a rich exchange of feelings. Talking in this way about work creates a kind of paradox: discussions about the office can prolong your feelings, but unspoken feelings may undermine your evening.

One couple, both entertainment executives, solve the problem by devoting 10 minutes to a game they call "How was your day at school?" Each person is allotted 5 minutes to talk about their day and the rest of the evening is devoted to other topics.

Once you have presented the edited version of your day, it will be your turn to listen.

5

"Let Me Give You Some Advice..."

I once toured Taliesin West, Frank Lloyd Wright's former residence/school in Arizona, where our tour guide relished telling a tale about the lady of the house. It seems that one afternoon, Frank was working in his studio and Mrs. Wright wandered in. He showed her a set of architectural drawings in progress and she was pointedly critical of the decisions he had made. Frank disagreed with her unsolicited critique and, shortly after, drove into town. During his absence, Mrs. Wright, who was not trained as an architect, went back to his studio and revised the drawings. Our guide smiled and informed us that Frank returned from town and found that her advice had been excellent; her revisions were just what the drawings needed!

Mrs. Wright's apocryphal intrusion is a perfect example of our most common response when we listen to loved ones talk about work: we give advice. In this case, Mrs. Wright went one step further and actually put her advice into practice. Although her architect husband was ultimately pleased with the results, his initial irritation should not be overlooked.

This story illustrates how problems can occur when we offer advice before recognizing what the recipient feels or needs. Like Mrs. Wright, we assume that the best way to demonstrate interest and concern is to give advice. But this is not always the case. As a listener, your priority should be to recognize feelings before offering solutions. Remember that the best advice is offered by invitation only.

Consider five questions we all ask instead of recognizing feelings about work.

FIVE FREQUENT BUT FRUSTRATING QUESTIONS

We often ask these questions when listening to tales about work. Each question frustrates, rather than encourages, the expression of feelings.

Question 1: "Why Don't You Quit?"

Carla L., a financial analyst, had suddenly, inexplicably, become the target of a whispering campaign. When she walked into the conference room, conversation stopped. Colleagues who had been friendly offered only a cursory hello.

When she first noticed the problem, Carla was confused and hurt. She needed to sort out her feelings and try to map out a plan of action. After several days, she sat down to explain her feelings to her husband, Gary. His response: "If it's really getting that bad, *why don't you quit?*" His question, though asked out of a genuine love and concern, derailed Carla from sorting out her feelings.

Gary offered the ultimate advice without exploring Carla's point of view; Gary's question marked the end of one conversation and the beginning of another. Carla was suddenly forced to justify remaining in a difficult job situation. She had been steered away from discussing her feelings about the whispering campaign. Instead, she launched into an explanation of how hard it would be to find another job and how the loss of salary would cause financial problems. Carla may eventually want to consider leaving her job. But, before she is ready to discuss such options, she needs to express her thoughts and feelings to Gary.

Before giving advice, Gary should have recognized Carla's strong feelings. As one hospital administrator explained, "I can't really solve work problems at home. I don't want advice. I don't want to debate. I want to talk about how I feel."

This distinction between men's desire for "report talk" and women's need for "rapport talk" is elegantly explained by sociologist Deborah Tannen in her book, *You Just Don't Understand.*

Later, you'll practice the skill of paraphrasing feelings as a prelude to giving advice. The guiding principle is the order of your responses: feelings demand your first recognition.

Question 2: "You Are Not Going to Do/Say That, Are You?"

As most people who talk to you about work are not aware of the five editing tools described in the previous chapter, you may find yourself listening to some unedited venting of the Mount Vesuvius variety. The rule of thumb is to take venting seriously, but not *literally*. Todd K., a dentist, describes the problem.

> *Sometimes Marie takes my feelings too seriously. She will pick me up in the car and I'll start complaining about my young associate. That arrogant SOB, I'm going to tell him . . . Marie will get this look of panic on her face and ask me, "You're not going to say that, are you?"*

As you listen to someone ventilate about work, you are providing companionship. A corporate vice president explains why this is important: "There are such strong political implications of confiding in someone at work; I have to be so controlled at work. With George, I want to ventilate my true feelings."

But you don't want to encourage unchecked ventilation. When you practice paraphrasing, you will find that recognizing feelings *reduces*, rather than increases, the possibility that someone will actually carry out a verbal or physical threat at work.

Question 3: "Do You Know What I'd Do?"

When you listen to someone expressing strong feelings about work, the most natural response is to associate their experience with something that happened to you. Your connection with your own experience may be a sincere attempt to understand, but your good intentions may be interpreted as a *failure* to understand.

When your husband is in the throes of a story about work, he feels that his situation is unique. If you listen and compare his situation with yours, he will think that you don't really understand. Later in the conversation, your advice, based on a similar experience, may be helpful. But to begin, you need to validate his feelings.

Responding with similar stories of your own, even in an attempt to show empathy, can often convey both one-upmanship and unsolicited advice.

> *He:* She did it again. She stared out her window during the entire meeting!
>
> *You:* You think that's bad. I had a client once who did his paperwork while we were talking. I finally told him that if he was too busy to meet, we could reschedule. *Do you know what I'd do?* I'd tell your client the same thing.

It might be helpful to share similar experiences, but wait for the person to ask for your perspective. Later, we will talk about the role your advice can play in conversations about work.

Now, try to recognize feelings first.

Question 4: "Why Do You Need to Talk About It?"

Jeanne H., a television news director, is familiar with this question. "Art thinks I talk too much. He can't understand why I need to think and process my feelings out loud. He tends to work things out on his own, so he always asks me, 'Why do you need to talk about it?'"

You may be like Art, who reviews and revises his feelings about the day on the freeway or on the tennis court. When you come home, you cherish a respite from discussions about work, and you resent another person's need to continue to talk about the day.

Questioning someone's need to talk about work will not reduce the number of words per minute; your question is likely to produce even *more* talk. When Art questions the validity of Jeanne's feelings about work, she is likely to talk with increased intensity and to exaggerate her feelings. She will try to justify, in the strongest possible terms, why her feelings are worthy of discussion.

If you don't want to listen to an extended replay of someone's day, practice paraphrasing. Once Art recognizes and validates Jeanne's feelings, she will feel relieved, and will be ready to move on to other topics and other activities.

Question 5: "Why Do You Take It So Seriously?"

Your husband tells you, "I am really worried. I have only three weeks to create a complete promotional campaign for our client." You take one look at his pinched face and wish that he wouldn't take his work so seriously. You are tempted to say, "Oh, don't worry, you have time. After all, Handel wrote the whole *Messiah* in 24 days." This attempt at humor may create a paradoxical effect; he may become even more serious as he attempts to convince you of the concerns he tried to laugh away.

Your first response as a listener can't be one of cheerful denial. If you smile and ask, *"Why do you take it so seriously?"* he will feel that you are trying to distract him or to deny that he has a problem. Instead, try recognizing his feelings with a simple restatement. "You are wondering if three weeks will be long enough to create a first-rate campaign." When you paraphrase his feelings, you allow him to begin smiling, on his own time schedule.

Have you had enough of those frustrating conversations? Let's see if the act of recognizing feelings lives up to its buildup as we take a closer look at the art of paraphrasing.

LEARNING FRENCH

Irwin Shaw's *The Man Who Married a French Wife* makes a charming case for the importance of recognizing another person's world.

The narrator of the story is a man revisiting Paris with the French wife he married during World War II. During their long marriage, he has never taken the time to learn French or to understand his wife's heritage. His wife introduces him to her former lover, a revolutionary. As the narrator learns of her past involvements in love and politics, he realizes how little time he has taken to understand her personal history or her point of view. As the story ends, the man is taking a thoughtful, hot bath and asks, "I wonder if it is too late for me to learn French?"

It is seldom "too late" to learn the language that describes the experiences of a friend or lover. When you listen to talk about work, "learning French" means that you try to understand a person's experiences at work in his or her own terms.

I'd like to reintroduce the art of *paraphrasing* as a kind of translation check: you'll learn to restate what someone is telling you, to check if you have understood their perspective about work.

I say reintroduce because, unfortunately, the subtle art of paraphrasing became the "fast food" of psychology back in the early 1970s. Paraphrasing was then the cliché of every media psychologist and was often introduced with silly opening lines like "If I catch your meaning" or "I hear you saying." So annoying was this glib application of a subtle art, that I used to threaten to fine my psychology students a nickel every time they used one of those openers!

Despite its overexposure and underutilization, paraphrasing remains the single most effective communication skill in listening to talk about work. When you practice paraphrasing as you listen to stories about work, you restate what you have heard to indicate that you have understood both the situation and the feelings involved.

Paraphrasing, as the five frustrating questions indicate, is most useful as a *first* response to work talk. It can set the climate for a comfortable conversation, help create a nonjudgmental atmosphere, and reduce defensiveness.

When you paraphrase, you silently ask yourself two questions: What is the situation? How does she/he feel about the situation?

When you attempt to understand a situation at work, you may be asked to follow a long story.

DETECTIVE'S WORK /
THE LONG STORY

Most people have strong feelings about difficult personalities and complicated situations at work. Unfortunately, when friends and family talk about these situations, they may not have organized their thoughts. In many cases, it would take a detective to follow some of the stories you will hear about life at the office.

When listening to long stories, take advantage of an amusing fact: You can listen two to three times faster than someone else can talk. Theoretically, then, you could use your "extra time" to mentally outline and answer the question "What *is* the situation she or he is describing?"

For inspiration to answer the question, look to the classic work of television's most famous sleuths, one a detective and the other an attorney: "Lieutenant Columbo," played memorably by Peter Falk, and "Perry Mason," the alter-ego of actor Raymond Burr.

TECHNIQUE:
Columbo's Conclusions

By the time Lieutenant Columbo arrived on the scene in his rumpled raincoat, we already knew who the murderer was. Virtually all of the episodes of "Columbo" began by showing the murder and identifying the murderer. As viewers following the storyline, we knew the *conclusions* of Columbo's investigation before we knew the *facts* of the case.

Listening to some people talk about work is like watching an episode of "Columbo." Like this physician talking about a series of job interviews, they will tell you their conclusions and then offer the details or facts of the story.

> *We finally decided to hire Dr. Riley. After interviewing 15 candidates in three days, we narrowed it down to Riley and Dr. Edwards. Both had fine training and recommendations; but we felt that Riley's background in public relations would be good for the clinic.*

People who offer the punch line, or the bottom line, first are the easiest to follow. Once they have stated their conclusions, you can do what Columbo did: Listen for the *facts* to fully understand the situation.

Other, more trying storytellers save the conclusions for *last*.

TECHNIQUE:
Building the Case

If you watched "Perry Mason," you never knew until the last 5 minutes, when Mason and District Attorney Burger were nose to nose, who actually committed the murder.

Mason and Burger took turns unfolding the case. As viewers, we listened patiently to the details of each case: the terms of the will and the condition of the body; the time the mail arrived and the time the suspect arrived. We were rewarded for our perseverance when Perry Mason pointed to the murderer in court and restated how he arrived at his conclusions. If you still didn't understand, the conclusions were reviewed in those famous posttrial lunches attended by Paul Drake and Della Street.

Listening to a friend talk about work can be as grueling as watching an episode of Perry Mason. You may have a loved one who relishes all of the detailed *facts* and saves the *conclusions* for last.

> *First we interviewed Dr. Morris from Dallas. He had a fine record and it turns out he even went to medical school with one of the selection committee . . . . On Tuesday, we interviewed five more people . . . . Then we narrowed it down to Dr. Riley and Dr. Edwards. It seemed that they both had fine training and good recommendations . . . . But we felt that Riley's background in public relations would be good for the clinic. We finally decided to hire Riley.*

If you can stand the suspense, keep track of the facts and listen carefully for the conclusions. If the wait becomes intolerable, you can say, "I'm getting lost. Can you tell me the punchline and then fill in the details?"

You can understand complicated work situations by mentally mapping the details and conclusions. You'll be ready to paraphrase once you've discovered the *feelings* that the situation evoked.

TECHNIQUE:
Listening to Feelings

The physician who interviewed 15 candidates and selected one will have some strong feelings about his involvement in the selection process. If you want to recognize and paraphrase his feelings, you need to listen carefully. He may feel relieved or tired; he may feel a sense of accomplishment or a feeling of disappointment. Your goal as a listener is to understand how this situation has affected him.

When someone tells you a story about work, ask yourself, "How does he or she really feel about this?" Consider these choices: afraid, amused, angry, annoyed, anxious, apprehensive, ashamed, assured, bored, burned, cautious, concerned, confident, confused, cornered, crushed, depressed, disappointed, disgusted, disillusioned, elated, embarrassed, empty, enthusiastic, envious, frustrated, furious, gratified, guilty, grieving, harassed, hopeful, hostile, humiliated, hurt, indignant, isolated, listless, miserable, overlooked, panicky, paralyzed, powerless, rejected, relieved, resentful, sad, skeptical, spiteful, successful, surprised, suspicious, tense, threatened, unappreciated, uncertain, uneasy.

When you paraphrase, you don't want to overstate the feelings you have heard; you want to remember the shading of feeling we talked about in Chapter 4.

NOT NECESSARILY A BULL'S-EYE

After you have identified feelings and attached them to a specific situation, you are ready to paraphrase. Follow these four steps to recognize and restate someone's perspective about work.

* Try to get inside the person's frame of reference. Ask yourself, "What is the basic feeling he or she is expressing? What is the situation or reason that evoked the feeling?"
* Restate the person's feelings and reasons in your own words.

- Observe a cue from the other person that shows you have accurately restated his or her perspective.
- If not, try again.

When you paraphrase, you fill in two blanks. The written form of a paraphrasing statement would look like this: My friend feels _____ _____.

In the following example, a friend has just received the news that his mentor in the investment firm is taking a job in another city:

He: After five years of getting Tom's best advice, I'm going to be left to fend for myself.

You: I can see that you are really going to feel a void when he leaves. (*restates feeling*) He's been one terrific guardian angel! (*restates situation*)

He: You're right; sometimes I felt like he was the only person in the firm who really gave a damn about what happened to me. (*confirms that your paraphrase was on target*)

Your paraphrasing may not always hit the bull's-eye, but your goal is to let the person know you understand. If you misread a feeling, the other person can get you back on target. Let's return to the friend who is losing a mentor.

You: It sounds like you are really *scared* about Tom leaving.

He: Not *scared* really, maybe a little *anxious.* I don't know what that place will be like without Tom's helpful hints.

Don't worry about being "right," you'll have many opportunities to communicate your willingness to understand.

If you feel you need more practice, a renowned family therapist has an idea for you.

TECHNIQUE:
"What Do You Mean?"

Family therapist Virginia Satir suggests that paraphrasing can be practiced by playing a short game of questions.

Begin by sitting down and listening to a friend or family member tell you a story. Listen carefully and after they have finished, ask them a series of questions to restate basic feelings and reasons, for example, "Do you mean that you felt _____

because_____?"

Keep asking questions until you get three "yeses."

If paraphrasing doesn't seem to fit your style, remember that you can show a strong presence and recognition in few or no words at all.

TECHNIQUE:
Winking, Blinking, and Nodding

"When I tell my husband about my work, he doesn't say or do anything until I finish talking. I wish he would grunt or nod or *something*. I become distracted, wondering what he is thinking," complains Shirley G., a systems engineer.

Nonverbal signs of encouragement are the essential acts of an empathic listener. Nodding, smiling, winking, or leaning forward while a story is in progress are all ways of saying, "I'm listening; I'm following."

Some communication experts suggest that your facial expressions should mirror the tone of what the other person is saying. You can take your cue from the person talking to you: if she is laughing, you can smile; if he is frowning, you can nod and frown slightly or wrinkle your nose. You can add small verbal phrases of encouragement to remind the person of your interest. Little phrases like "um-hmm . . . ," "go on," and "I see" are short but sweet signs to the person seeking your undivided attention.

These nonverbal gestures and brief encouragements indicate your willingness to withhold judgment and recognize the person's immediate feelings before offering your advice.

THE BEST ADVICE

When you recognize the feelings of family and friends through encouragement and paraphrase, you establish a climate for mutual problem solving. In this atmosphere, advice is best offered by invitation only.

Practice two techniques to initiate the process of moving beyond feelings about work to the solution of work-related problems.

TECHNIQUE:
Brainstorming

A favorite technique of organizational consultants, *brainstorming* is a process by which participants suggest every possible solution to a problem without evaluating them. This process allows the group to "think out loud," to consider unconventional possibilities in a safe atmosphere.

Brainstorming can initiate the process of problem solving in conversations about work. Begin with a simple question: *"Have you thought about your options?"* This technique is most effective when you have recognized the feelings involved. Carla L., the financial analyst concerned with whispering colleagues, is a case in point. Her husband, Gary, listened to her story and offered her an immediate option: he suggested she quit. His alternative was to recognize and paraphrase Carla's feelings of confusion and hurt. Once he had established his understanding of her perspective, he might have asked about her options.

Rather than suggesting options, let the other person "brainstorm" by listing the possibilities that come to her mind. As a listener, you should withhold judgment and simply restate the options as you continue to explore possibilities.

Carla and Gary's brainstorming session could have sounded like this:

Gary: It all sounds so confusing, like you don't really have a clue about how this whispering got started. (*paraphrases*)

Carla: Yeah, I'm completely stumped. (*confirms his paraphrase was accurate*)

Gary: Have you had a chance to think about your options for getting to the bottom of this? (*doesn't demand answers or offer advice; simply opens the discussion*)

Carla: I was thinking about asking Burt; he has always been honest with me. But if *he* is involved in the problem, I wouldn't want to give him any ammunition. (*states an option and her own objection*)

Gary: So Burt is a possibility, but you're not even sure that you trust him. (*restates option and objection; doesn't evaluate or give advice*)

If Carla and Gary continue to brainstorm, Carla will have the opportunity to think out loud with the benefit of Gary's empathic companionship. She is likely to arrive at a plan of action as a result of their discussion. Before the discussion ends, Carla may ask Gary for his advice. Advising, when preceded by paraphrasing and brainstorming, can be a marvelous way to communicate that you have been listening.

Once again, the important factor is that you recognize feelings first and that your advice is requested.

Let's reconsider the Taliesin tall tale about Frank Lloyd Wright in terms of the technique of advice by consent.

TECHNIQUE:
The Wrights Revisited

Mrs. Wright could have offered her infamous advice in a less intrusive manner. She could have asked her architect husband a simple question: "Do you want my opinion?"

Let's say that the drawings in question were of a residence to be built on ocean-front property in California, and that she thought that the living room facing the ocean didn't have enough windows. If he had invited her critique, she could have followed three rules for giving advice with consent.

- Acknowledge your limitations. Recognize the fact that you are offering an opinion that lacks the background and experience in the other person's field.

   Mrs. W.: I know I'm not an architect, but if I were sitting in that living room, I would want more windows and more of an ocean view.

- Once you have stated your opinion, don't press your point. If the other person disagrees, don't debate; paraphrase their point of view.

Mr. W.:   Yes, but in the evening after the sun goes down, you would look out and see a big, dark, and blank space; you couldn't see the ocean. I decided to put this fireplace on the ocean wall to provide a warm focus in the evening.

Mrs. W.:   So you have thought about the windows, but decided that it was more important to reduce the dark outlook.

• Don't become invested in your opinion or advice. Offer your perspective and indicate your interest in the other person's decision.

Mrs. W.:   It is an interesting problem. I'd love to see the rest of the drawings when you finish.

Endless conversations about work will extend the workday long into the night. If you can enjoy satisfying, *time-limited* dialogues about the day, you'll be able to use the remaining hours for self-renewal.

PART THREE

Paths to Renewal

6

To Work and to Love

She is one of those women who preside over perfume commercials—a lovely woman dressed in a gray flannel suit, pearls, and pumps. She is obviously a powerful woman because the three men at the table are listening intently to her.

The narrator almost whispers his comment: "From a distance, she is *discreet, elegant.*"

The camera then cuts to another scene with the same woman. She appears, *sans* suit and bare-shouldered, enjoying some tiny kisses on her neck from a man who was definitely *not* at the business lunch!

Now the punch line: "But up close, she is *something else.*"

In its own silly way, the scent ad plays on our rich fantasies about the transition from work to love. It celebrates the distant and discreet cool we project in our professional relationships, and reminds us of how we all hope to be "something else" with the people we meet after work.

Unfortunately, the "something else" we become at the end of the day is not nearly as delightful as those tiny kisses might suggest.

The transition from work to love captures the true meaning of Bogart's classic toast, "Here's looking at *you.*" Intimacy demands that you turn your attention away from yourself and your work, and focus on the loving presence of your partner. This transition requires time and patience. From the moment you arrive, you will be struggling to protect your time together from the problems of your day at work.

FROM SHOPTALK TO
SWEET-TALK

Talking and listening to feelings about work are the foundation of a cozy evening at home. When you can acknowledge anger, disappointment, and fears, you become vulnerable, more open to your intimate feelings. As you recognize the feelings of your mate, you indicate your willingness to become a receptive, empathic partner.

It takes an enormous amount of energy to withhold and hide feelings about work, and the feelings rarely remain hidden. Consider two scenarios in which feelings about work appear in a disguised form. In each case, they interfere with the growth of trust and comfort in the relationship.

Hidden Failures

I will never forget my lunch with Ken R., an attorney whose practice had failed to prosper. He was exhausted and depressed and talked about declaring bankruptcy. "How does Ellen feel about all this?" I asked. Ken shifted in his chair and answered, "She doesn't know." Nor can I forget a spectacular shouting match between Ken and Ellen on the balcony of their rented apartment on Martha's Vineyard. "I hate you," screamed Ken, within earshot of hundreds of people on the beach.

Marriage is not an arena for "keeping up a good front." Ken may have hidden his business failures from his legal colleagues, but he should have confided them to his wife. Instead, he borrowed money, juggled funds, and became hopelessly overextended on his credit cards. He tried "hinting" to Ellen, and eventually resented her for "not guessing."

Talking about fears and failures allows you to express a vulnerability that is *the* prerequisite for intimacy. Ken could have shared his financial burdens with Ellen. When he chose to hide his failures, he created a wall of resentment, and both of them lost the opportunity to deepen their relationship during the difficult times.

Frozen Anger

Mary Anne L., a telecommunications manager, came home after finding out that one of her employees had gone over her head to reverse a decision she had made. She was determined not to ruin the evening by talking about it. Her husband, Daniel, asked about her day and she offered a vague description.

As the evening continued, Mary Anne found herself involved in a series of minibattles with Dan: "Why hadn't he fed the cats? Why did they *have* to visit his parents this weekend?" When they got into bed and Dan moved closer, she said angrily, "I'm just not in the mood; couldn't you tell?"

Dan began a gentle, probing conversation with Mary Anne and they were able to connect the source of her anger. By the time they finished talking, they were too tired to make love, but they fell asleep with their arms around each other.

When you state your anger or frustration about work, you clear the path for more affectionate and sexual expression.

After all of your careful and caring conversations about work, you'll be ready to change the subject. The transition from work to love can be graced by a rich exchange of feelings and appreciations.

TECHNIQUE:
The Next Subject

Sandra and David P. work together in a hospital laboratory, doing groundbreaking scientific research. "My husband could talk about work constantly if I didn't stop him," said Sandra. "One night, I was fixing dinner and he began to talk to me about the results of today's tests. I got very angry and told him, 'You must stop this; I cannot talk about science 24 hours a day.'"

She reports that they now have imposed a rule of a brief work-related conversation and then a change of subject. "We really enjoy talking about the people we know, what they are doing, what makes them tick."

Mona and John B. moved to Los Angeles to accept high-pressure jobs in the entertainment business. In their first months, they talked about work throughout dinner every night. After six months, they set some limits. They set aside 15 minutes to debrief news about "the business" and then, says Mona, "we like to talk about the kind of life we are living; whether we want to have children or buy a house, or whether our values have changed since we moved here."

Talking about work can be a symptom of work stress or a sign of a relationship without shared interests. Sometimes talk about work is an escape from silence or boredom.

Make a practice of changing the subject. If you and your partner are in a rut and continuously talk about work, try the variety of other topics of conversation: presidential politics, family (yours, mine, and ours), good news about friends, the book or magazine article you are reading, whether to vacation in Mexico, see Oliver Stone's latest movie, buy a home computer, or join the Sierra Club.

As you shift the focus away from your concern about work, you'll be able to express your appreciation of each other. Compliments and thank-you notes can be a delightful change of subject.

TECHNIQUE:
"Let Me Count the Ways."

Time at home provides the opportunity to look at your partner in emotional, appreciative terms. You don't have to be a poet to "count the ways" in which your partner delights you. But you may have difficulty translating your feelings of appreciation into words. In your search for a fitting compliment, ask yourself two questions:

• If you ran into a friend who hadn't seen you in 10 years, and had never met your partner, how would you describe him or her?

• If you wrote a profile of your partner as a most unforgettable character, what qualities would you emphasize?

As you begin to discover the depth of your appreciation for your partner, develop the habit of sharing your sweet and loving appreciation of them. The key is specificity. Rather than saying "You are really generous," say "I love watching your face light up when you pick up the tab for dinner with friends."

Practice accepting compliments. When your wife tells you how generous you are, stifle your impulse to deny it. Catch yourself, smile, and reply, "What a nice thing to say."

TECHNIQUE:
Thank-you Notes

"Thank you" can be the sweetest phrase at the end of the day. Each one of us thrives on the feeling of being appreciated, and intimates are well advised to practice the art of sending verbal thank-you notes.

Develop the habit of appreciating your partner's thoughtful words and deeds:

• Be specific: mention time and place. Don't say "You are really good to me." Instead, try "Last night, when you talked to me about my supervisor, you really helped me figure out what to do. Thanks for listening to me rattle on and on about it."

• Stay current. Try to mention your appreciation within 24 hours. Thank-you's lose their punch over time. "That was a wonderful dinner you planned for my mother tonight" has more appeal than "I have been meaning to thank you for the way you made Mom's birthday so special last week."

You'll also want to talk about plans for your time after work. To do this, eliminate the task orientation that motivates you during the workday.

FROM PURPOSEFUL
TO PLAYFUL

You race through the workday, returning phone calls, dictating letters, and meeting with colleagues, clients, students, or patients. You set priorities, make decisions, and solve problems. Efficiency is the greatest asset during business hours. After work, a sense of purpose can reduce spontaneity.

The Management Mode

When you make the transition between work and love, the task orientation of the day can diminish the prospects of a playful or sexy time at home.

Claudia and Tim F., a busy professional couple, realized that they were depriving themselves of time off from work. Claudia explained, "On Saturday morning, we'd start with our list: rake leaves, fix storm windows, do laundry, shop for groceries. We used to make love in the afternoons; now, we are too efficient. We get into our 'management mode' and spend the day finishing tasks. We don't even get *near* the bedroom."

It is important to turn off the work habit of overscheduling time. Intimacy is established at a slower, more spontaneous pace. You'll need to postpone the sense of "purpose" that motivates you during working hours.

You might start by changing your name.

TECHNIQUE:
"Who's Pinkie?"

In the movie *Adam's Rib,* Katharine Hepburn and Spencer Tracy were the epitome of a glamorous two-career couple. These two attorneys meshed beautifully until the day they faced each other in court.

In a hilarious courtroom scene, they confounded the judge by referring to each other by a private nickname: "It wasn't that way at all, Pinkie," said Hepburn for-the-defense. "That's what you think, Pinkie," said Tracy for-the-prosecution. "Who's Pinkie?" asked the judge.

Private nicknames are the way that many couples draw the line between professional and intimate conversations. One physician is Dr. Matthews by day, and "Gumby" at night. His wife calls him Gumby because he is tall, slim, and very limber in bed!

Nicknames are the result of the private conversations and shared experiences of a couple. Pet names should be silly, sexy, and fun. They are a definite reminder that you have come home from work. But you may need more than a reminder.

The Overplanned Vacation

Lisa and Patrick D. looked forward to their spring trip to Italy all winter. They had booked hotels, ground tours, and opera tickets months in advance. Somewhere between Venice and Florence, they began to feel exhausted. The itinerary they had so carefully planned and booked in advance was interfering with their enjoyment of each other. They would set their alarm, rise early, and tackle the second floor of the Uffizi Gallery. As each evening arrived, they would drag themselves to sit through a prebooked concert or play and return to the hotel, too tired to make love.

They finally decided to cancel some of their plans and take a lesson from their Italian hosts, a people famous for their capacity to savor the sights, sounds, and smells around them.

At work, we are oriented toward a linear progression of events: If we finish A, we can proceed to B. Playful, sensual time has no "goal" other than the enjoyment of all of your senses.

TECHNIQUE:
Smell the Pizza

In most jobs, we try to shut out the stimulation of our senses so that we can concentrate; we receive most information through our eyes and ears. Intimate relationships thrive on awakening the neglected senses of touch, taste, and smell.

On your way home from work, make an effort to reconnect with rich sensory experiences: Walk past an Italian restaurant and smell the pizza. Stop at a fruit stand and bite into a crisp, fragrant apple; feel your silk slip brush against your legs; blink the raindrops from your eyelashes.

Jean Houston, author of *The Possible Human,* asked a group of her friends to list their most pleasurable sensory experiences. You might want to join your partner in summoning forgotten sensory delights, for example, a summer sky during a meteor shower, riding through a light snowfall with your convertible top down, the cologne you wore in high school, a chocolate soda with chocolate ice cream.

Sweet, confiding conversation and sensory enjoyment allow you to anticipate the pleasure of making love after work, that is, if you can keep your preoccupation with goals out of the bedroom.

FROM PRESSURE
TO PLEASURE

Making love can be the celebration, if not the focus, of genuine intimacy. Sexual love is a precious opportunity for both the physical release of stress and emotional renewal. It is also, as one attorney admits, "the first thing to go" when the pressures of work add up and the problems of fatigue, unfinished business, and self-absorption stand in the way of intimacy and arousal.

When you practice techniques to review and share your feelings about work, you have taken the first steps toward becoming emotionally available. If you can switch from a task orientation to a sensual and playful focus, you remove another obstacle to intimacy.

The final obstacle involves removing the concern with performance from your experience of sexual love.

Sex by Objectives

It makes good business sense to set a series of professional objectives for yourself and for the people you manage. It is pure madness to be concerned with your "goals and performance" in bed.

When you say, "I'm too tired," you may be speaking in code. You may really mean that you're too tired to have multiple orgasms or to search for your G-spot. You might enjoy cuddling or a less-than-transcendental sexual encounter, but you have set other goals for yourself. You might actually feel that orgasms are highly overrated at the end of an exhausting day, that you would enjoy sharing other sexual play with your partner, but you think that *she* has other goals in mind.

The joy of a sexual relationship after work is sharing warm moments together and you can plan to share some kind of sexual experience together every day. You can enjoy moments of fantasy and touch that allow you to stay connected to each other's sexual self.

I won't even use the word *technique* in this section; the key is an experience of sexual play that is not oriented toward specific goals. The approaches that follow can initiate delightful sexual encounters after work.

1. Undress for Success

Dressed in jeans and crew-necked sweaters, Claudia and Tim F. sat in my office talking about their difficulties in leaving behind the "management mode" they both carried home from work.

Claudia said she had the most trouble leaving her goals behind. She paused thoughtfully, and I found myself wondering about the clothes she wore to work. I asked her to describe her work clothes to Tim. How did she feel when she wore them?

"I always wear a dark suit with a high-collared blouse, plain pumps, and very little jewelry. I work hard at hiding any hint of sexiness. When I come home, I feel very tight and buttoned down, not very responsive."

The act of changing clothes is an important ritual for most people at the end of the day. For many couples, the experience of undressing together becomes an integral part of sexual play.

One couple occasionally plays strip poker before drifting off to sleep. Another begins every heart-to-heart talk by taking off their clothes. Other couples take long, soapy showers together.

The act of "turning in her suit" had significance for Claudia and she began to use the change of clothes to create a different picture of herself after work. She and Tim began to plan deliberate rituals, like enjoying a glass of wine together to create a more intimate homecoming.

2. Teenage Thrills

Ron, a stockbroker, confided in me: "When my wife and I were first dating, we used to spend these long evenings just kissing and holding each other. It was wonderful; I felt just like a teenager!" He wistfully concluded, "Now, we just jump straight into bed."

Remember back seats and drive-in movies and the front porch? Those "make-out" sessions seemed to last for hours, with the promise that "maybe next time . . ." You can enjoy the thrills of a teenager's anticipation of sex. Even when you feel "too tired" to make love, you can still enjoy some long, sweet kisses and lingering caresses.

"Next time" will arrive soon enough.

3. Fantasyland

Walt Disney can't be your guide to this approach, but shared fantasies (not acted on) can be an alternative for exhausted participants. You can stimulate your imaginations, if not your bodies.

* Think about a change in location. "I'd like to be sitting in a cafe in Paris with you, on the way to our tiny room on the Rue des Ecole."

* Share memories of your greatest hits. "Remember the night of Nancy's wedding?"

* Make promises you can keep. "Let's sleep in tomorrow and have breakfast in bed."

James Thurber summed up the essence of pure enjoyment of sexual feelings, *without* objectives, when he said, "I love the idea of there being two sexes, don't you?"

A QUESTION OF INTIMACY

Denise S., a very composed physician, slid into the chair next to mine at a community meeting. In the middle of a rather mild conversation, she blurted, "Paul and I have been so busy, we just haven't made love in over a month!"

The pressures and demands of work can contribute to the escalation of a situation like Denise's. Each partner comes home fatigued, self-absorbed, and irritable; these are not the feelings that contribute to shared intimacy after work.

The approaches in this chapter can offer delightful options for intimate encounters. But if you begin to feel that even these playful options are "a chore," there may be more to your avoidance of intimate contacts than your tyrannical boss. Concerns about work can cover for unspoken anger or anxiety about the relationship itself. If you sense this problem, sit down with your partner and explore your feelings together.

Begin by expressing your feelings about the loss of intimate times together. Ask your partner's help in uncovering anger, resentment, or anxiety in your relationship. Are either of you upset about children, in-laws, housework, money, lack of appreciation, or the division of labor or power in the relationship? Are unspoken feelings clouding your time together and causing you to use work as a smokescreen? Question each other tenderly about work and about feelings in your relationship that may keep you from enjoying the renewal to be found in your intimate connection.

Remind each other of Dr. Freud's famed definition of health: When asked what a "normal" person should be able to do well, Freud simply said, "*Lieben und arbeiten* [to love and work]."

7

The Friendship Factor

*I*n the winter of 1924, Harold Loeb invited Ernest and Hadley Hemingway to a lobster dinner at the Nègre de Toulouse in Paris. Loeb couldn't have imagined that two years later he would be humiliated when his friends recognized him as the model for the passive Robert Cohn in *The Sun Also Rises*.

Hemingway's biographer, Carlos Baker, reported that Hemingway developed quite a reputation for using his friends as models for the characters in his novels. Mr. Loeb was neither the first nor the last subject of Hemingway's devastating caricatures.

It could be argued that all writers transform their relationships within their work, but Hemingway was known for viewing his friendships as "fair game." And my queasiness with Hemingway's betrayal of his "cafe society" extends to other working professionals who contaminate their friendships with business styles and agendas.

Many professionals allow their friendships to walk a thin line between business and pleasure. Friendship becomes yet another arena to practice skills that are productive in professional life, but destructive to the growth of intimate relationships.

Friendship offers a precious opportunity to remove yourself from the competitive professional world. If you approach friendship with a business agenda, you lose the chance to cultivate a life separate from work.

Let me ask you some friendly questions: When you invite four couples over for dinner, do you run out to buy more place settings from your wedding pattern? Did you recently have dinner with a friend for the first time in three months and tell them how hard it was to "fit them in?" And finally, have you ever handed out business cards at a family wedding?

If you recognize yourself in these choices, you have intruded your business style into your precious time with friends. Let's explore three aspects of professional savvy that undermine friendship, and consider the possibilities for protecting friendships from your professional expertise.

MAKING AN IMPRESSION: A 24-HOUR JOB

The skill to create a "good impression" is the foundation of all successful business relationships. During the course of the workweek, we all struggle to project a polished, professional profile in the face of strong competition from colleagues.

The effort to achieve and maintain a good impression often persists after work. When this happens, you deprive yourself of the ultimate pleasure of intimacy: the chance to be relaxed, genuine, and cooperative. If you are scrambling to "look good," you won't have the chance to be silly or to tell bad jokes because it would tarnish your cool, professional veneer. You won't cultivate the kind of friends that you could call at three in the morning.

If you enter friendships determined to present a competitive business profile, you won't risk talking about your disappointments and your dreams. To open up possibilities for genuine intimacy, you need to abandon your desire to impress your friends.

Impression 1: "Cleaning Up for Company."

Many working people refuse to invite friends into their homes because "The house is a mess" or "We haven't had time to re-cover the sofa (buy six wine goblets, paint the dining room, or get guest towels for the bathroom)."

Friends who focus on making an impression at home have forgotten the purpose of extending an invitation. Remember, your friends come for the pleasure of your company, not to inspect the glasses for spots. The intimacy of your kitchen or dining-room table adds a dimension of enjoyment that is unavailable in even the most intimate restaurants.

If your real purpose is to enjoy your friends, you don't need the services of a maid or an interior decorator before extending an invitation. Practice asking yourself the following question.

TECHNIQUE:
"What's a Few Crumbs Among Friends?"

Rachelle B., a charming university official, reminds herself of the importance of friendship and the triviality of cleaning up for company. "I am a single parent with two kids. Our house stays clean for about five minutes at a time. When I get concerned about visiting friends, I simply tell myself, 'So, what's a few crumbs among friends?' "

Impression 2: "Cooking for Company."

Formal dinner parties may be appropriate for entertaining heads of state and chairmen of corporations. But do you really want friendships that depend on your dexterity in stuffing a Cornish game hen? You say "no," but why does the prospect of inviting your good friends David and Helene to dinner initiate the frenzied purchase of truffles, fresh basil, and designer pasta?

When the "company" is close friends, the idea is to create a relaxed atmosphere for an informal evening. You can't help others feel at ease if you are focused on whether or not the walnut sauce has thickened.

Elaborate menus can impair spontaneity in conversations. How many times have you had a dinner party where you spent the evening like a jack-in-the-box, jumping up every three minutes to check on the next course?

Remember, the priority of the evening should be conversation, not cuisine. After years of "cooking for company," I made an agreement with a friend.

TECHNIQUE:
Gourmet Armistice

One day at lunch I was talking to my friend Laura about how we had stopped inviting each other to dinner. And I decided to take the plunge. "I think one reason why we rarely invite each other is because we feel we have to make something special for dinner. By now, we know that all four of us are good cooks. What would happen if we agreed *"no more rack of lamb?"*

We laughed and talked about how we could plan more casual, less elaborate evenings together. We freed each other from the urge to "cook for company" by agreeing to some new patterns for spending time together.

Try some of these possibilities to plan for your own gourmet armistice.

- When a friend asks "Can I bring anything?" answer "Yes, how about dessert?" Potluck dinners don't mean you don't have the money to feed your friends; they allow you to share time together.

- Invite friends to help prepare a complicated recipe together. Spend the evening in the kitchen, drinking wine and exploring the mysteries of Cantonese cooking.

- Don't feel that everything must be ready before your friends ring the bell. Invite them into the kitchen and enjoy the conversation while you prepare dinner.

- Give up the idea that you must cook everything yourself. Buying breads, desserts, and salads allows you to cut your preparation time in half and to feel freer to invite guests at the last minute. Ask yourself, Will the evening really be less festive if I buy, rather than make, a Black Forest cake?

Other friends can vouch for the success of their armistices. Michelle H., a development officer, describes the essence of *enjoying*, rather than cooking for, company. "With everyone's crazy schedules, David and I treasure our time with Bill and Anna. We are thrilled to grab a pizza, bring it over to our house, and talk, talk, talk."

The exception is for those who find cooking a form of relaxation. If chopping garlic and separating egg whites are the acts of a soothing, relaxing hobby, you won't feel the pressures of the "bake-off" scenario.

If you are one of those rare people who delights in sharing a new inexpensive Chardonnay with friends, and can talk about it without stagy affect, continue to share your discoveries.

Just examine your motives carefully. If you are cooking and pouring to impress your friends, you are working too hard. Get out of the kitchen and get involved with your guests.

Impression 3: "We Couldn't Be Happier."

When you see your friend David kiss the tip of his wife Sharon's nose, your first thought may be, "I wonder if they make love more often than we do" or "Do *we* seem as happy/sexy as they do?"

It takes two to compete in this round; the goal is to impress your friends that you and your partner are the happiest couple in your circle. Have you been spending time with friends openly fondling your spouse, displaying your anniversary presents, or swearing that you never argue about household chores?

When you waste time with friends demonstrating your own happiness, you lose the opportunity to enjoy the warmth, trust, and silliness that couples can share. Dinner parties, picnics, and weekends at the beach can become a series of dance contests. All you would need is Dick Clark appearing from behind the bandstand to hold his hand over your head and say, "Let's hear it for couple number 1."

If your time with other couples is colored by competitive thoughts and observations, try to shift into a less competitive gear.

TECHNIQUE:
Second Thoughts

Maybe you will always have a first impulse to present your marriage in the best possible light. But your *second* thoughts can be less competitive.

When you see David kiss Sharon's nose, stop yourself from applying your lips directly to your partner's nose. Try to substitute a second set of less competitive thoughts:

"They seem happy; that's great."

"Slow down; this isn't the Newlywed Game."

"I enjoy having friends who are happy together."

When you catch yourself competing with close friends, refuse to compete. Focus your thoughts in another direction.

Impression 4: "Business Is Great!"

In the classic movie about downward mobility, *Fun with Dick and Jane,* we see a recently fired executive (George Segal) trying to impress a potential employer at dinner. The dinner, prepared by his wife (Jane Fonda), is expensive and elegant.

The point of the dinner was to hide the couple's desperation and to impress the employer with Dick's casual affluence. Meanwhile, during dinner, landscape contractors were outside removing trees and shrubs that the couple couldn't pay for.

It may be important to convince potential employers and clients that "business is good." With friends, this charade will deprive you of warmth and support during difficult times. You need to have at least one close friend to whom you can say, "Business is terrible; I'm holding my breath until the first of the month."

The struggle to appear successful during the workweek can become an exhausting deception with close friends. Examine your motives carefully. Does the desire to compete with close friends push you to give the impression that "business is great"?

TECHNIQUE:
The Real Story

I agree that it would be self-destructive to broadcast the details of your floundering business/career. But it is also destructive to keep the reality of your struggles to yourself.

Signs of competition during bad times include agreeing to meals, vacations, tickets, and events you can't afford. You'd rather be hounded by American Express than admit you can't afford to participate.

Hard times are lonely and scary; don't deepen the pain by pretending. If you pretend to maintain an impression or compete with friends, you will feel a chilling sense of isolation. Tell at least one friend the "real story" about your professional life. Allow a friend to demonstrate his or her concern and belief in you. You'll find that your friendships don't depend on your ability to rent a condo in Aspen during Christmas.

Refuse to participate in social gatherings you can't afford. Tell friends, "I'm on a lean and mean budget this month. The Four Seasons is out of the question."

Try to protect friendships from your skills in impression management and your skills in "managing time."

TIME MANAGEMENT: "BUSIER THAN THOU"

Time management is number 1 on the hit parade of corporate training classes. As a result, millions of working people walk through the day muttering about the need to prioritize.

Your ability to establish priorities and to manage your time on the job may be a key element in your successful career or business. When your preoccupation with time and efficiency extends to the hours after work, you can destroy the spontaneity and delight of time with friends.

Time with friends offers a different experience of time than the priorities you set on the job. Your friends will not be impressed with how busy you are, and they don't want to be "managed." As a friend, your profile may bear a strong resemblance to Alice's white rabbit tour guide in Wonderland, who was always "late for a very important date." When you talk to friends on the phone, you are "just on your way out." You can't get together next week because "you have been working too hard."

I am still cringing from my latest stumble into the rabbit hole and I appreciate my friend Ralph for pointing it out to me. We had plans for dinner when my sister unexpectedly flew in from Los Angeles. Instead of simply canceling our dinner plans, I said, "We could reschedule, but then I'd be out every night this week." Ralph told me later, "You know, I didn't mind you changing plans because of your sister, but when you told me about your whole *schedule*, I felt pretty unimportant."

Like Ralph, your friends may feel like clients that you are trying to "fit in." Or, you may have cultivated the bad habit of canceling dates with friends to accommodate the last-minute requests of bosses or business associates. It is important to spend playful time with friends that is free from the efficient management of your time. Consider creating and protecting special times for your friendships.

- Cultivate the habit of thinking of personal dates as carrying the same kind of commitment as business dates.

- Stop talking about how busy you are or where you have to go on Monday.

- Plan to occasionally say "no" to the last-minute requests of your boss and keep your date with a friend.

- Don't use the expressions "fit you in" and "booked" when making a date with a friend.

Friendships cannot flourish when intimates foster the value of staying "busier than thou." You'll need to separate and protect special time for your friends.

It is also essential to keep your circle of friends at a safe and separate distance from your "network" of professional associates.

THE DARKER SIDE OF NETWORKING

Your network of business contacts is the foundation of a lifelong career plan. As you cultivate the professional habit of "high visibility," you may begin to wonder where your business network ends and your friendships begin.

Diana K., a consultant I admire, describes the problem: "I was making up the guest list for my husband's birthday party and I noticed that I was inviting friends and business associates. I realized that I had broken a long-standing rule about not inviting business contacts into my home. I told myself that I was doing it for a 'higher good.' But what is the higher good?"

It would be easy to allow every dinner party, Easter Parade, wedding, or political fundraiser to become an opportunity to add new names to your professional network. You must be vigilant, or the same skills of networking that have enabled you to prosper in business will become the focus of *all* social occasions.

Perhaps it is unrealistic to think that business can be kept completely separate from the pleasure of your friendships. But, if you cherish the value of your time after work, you'll need to exercise self-control to eliminate scenarios that expose the darker side of networking.

Scenario 1: "Here's My Card."

Small-business owners and fast-track professionals are apt to line even the pockets of their ski parkas with business cards. They know that every occasion offers the opportunity to promote business or self and to add to a business network.

Gene, the owner of a fleet of florist services, admitted sheepishly, "I'm always looking for opportunities to pump up my business. Last week, my wife and I went to our first childbirth education class. Instead of getting to know the other people, I kept thinking, 'I've got to bring some business cards next time!'" Your business card is the symbol of the visibility and the network of powerful contacts you want to cultivate. The pursuit of visibility in social situations contaminates old and new friendships and robs you of the opportunity to draw a clear line between work and play.

Friendships and social events need to be experienced in an arena that is separate from the staging of your self-promotion. It is essential to learn when to be invisible, when to pull in your net.

TECHNIQUE:
Becoming Invisible

When Diana K. was planning her husband's birthday, she wondered, "Are all of my relationships utilitarian?" It takes practice to refrain from thinking of every conversation as a job interview and every person as a potential client. You can avoid the discomfort of "expedient" friendships in several ways:

During the Workweek

- Join several professional organizations specifically for the purpose of building your networks. Examine possibilities with cool, professional criteria, asking "Which group will provide the most connections for me?"

- Earmark several lunches, breakfasts, or dinner meetings during the work week to follow up on new and old business contacts.

After Work

- Leave business cards at home when you attend social occasions. If you must make note of a business contact at a friend's wedding, use a cocktail napkin. Remember, you are there as a friend, not as a professional.

- Refuse to elaborate on your professional interests at special celebrations (see Technique: The Assertive Cocktail, Chapter 8); change the subject and move on to more lighthearted topics.

Large celebrations can easily confuse business and friendly agendas.

Scenario 2: The Tax-Deductible Wedding

There are dreary affairs; the guest list is 50 percent clients, dress is conservative, the music is sedate, and spouses respond to sexual innuendos with vague smiles.

Try not to compromise the important milestones in your life by inviting your closest friends to mingle with your business associates. You may gain tax advantages, but you'll lose an opportunity to celebrate and take time off for wild behavior.

I urge you to distinguish between business functions and joyous celebrations. *Consider the following as business opportunities, opportunities to make an impression or build your network:* the company Christmas party, an associate's wedding, a retirement dinner, a professional association meeting, a convention, the office picnic. *Protect these events from your business agenda:* your golden anniversary, your son's bar mitzvah, your birthday, New Year's Eve.

TECHNIQUE:
Study the Guest List

"It's my party and I'll cry if I want to," sang Lesley Gore during a less complicated era.

Even with a broken heart, she had a good point. When you give a party, you should feel free to laugh, cry, or overeat. If you mix friends and clients at parties, you may be unable to ignore the presence of your network. You will feel pressured by the need to maintain your professional image. Afraid to appear "out of control" in front of your business associates, you'll deprive yourself of the opportunity to "cry if you want to," to learn new dance steps from your nephew, or to lip sync old Beatles songs.

One corporate vice president explained the pressure of socializing with business associates: "I would *never* invite business contacts to a special dinner party. It does absolutely nothing for my power woman image to be seen whipping up a soufflé in the kitchen."

When you plan a special party, limit the guest list to friends. With rare exceptions, your business associates do not care about you as a person. Their concern is with the business and services you can offer during working hours. Why include them at memorable occasions?

Draw a firm line between friendships cultivated for business and pleasure. You may lose the chance to gain a new client, but you gain the priceless time to enjoy friendships untouched by business concerns.

"DID YOU WORK THIS WEEKEND?"

My friend Peter describes a popular but defeating game that friends can play: "One of the reasons that I left Washington, D.C. was because of the emphasis on working overtime. No one ever asked, 'How was your weekend?' The question was: 'Did you *work* this weekend?' Working evenings and weekends was something that friends bragged about. It was like receiving a Purple Heart."

Friends can discourage one another from "working overtime" and extend an invitation to practice the art of self-renewal.

8

The Practice of Play

*C*onsider a scenario of two hard-working French scientists on the road to discovering radium. It seems that Pierre Curie was worried about Marie. One evening when she came home from the laboratory, he said to her: "You've worked long enough without a rest; you must take a vacation." "Where in the world would I go?" asked Marie. Suggested Pierre, "Pick the one place you would rather be, more than anywhere on earth." Marie promised, "I'll go tomorrow." The next morning, she was back at work in her laboratory.

Like these scientists, many of us need lessons in the art of self-renewal. We all complain that we "don't have enough time" away from work, but how are you spending your precious leisure time? Is your time an extension of work, tackling a "to do" list a mile long, or do you use leisure for experiences that are refreshing, stimulating, and rejuvenating?

To discover patterns in your free time, use one of two methods:

- List activities you have enjoyed during the last three months. Did they take place during the week or weekend? Were they solo activities or done with friends or family? Was the goal relaxation, stimulation, adventure, community involvement, entertainment, personal growth, physical fitness?

- Dr. Gerald Forester, a University of Washington psychologist, suggests that you carry a packet of 3 x 5 cards for a week and make a note, on a different card, each time you change activities.

This approach can give you an overview of your work/after-work activities. Make a special note of job-related activities: Do you extend your work skills and habits into your free time or do you compensate by doing something very different?

As you recall and list your activities, you may begin to recognize a definite style to the way you spend your time after work. Do you recognize one of these patterns?

"TGIF"

The five-day workweek has inspired almost as much graffiti as sex on the walls of subways, bus stations, and bathrooms around the world. A chain of restaurants called "TGIF" are packed every night, after five.

The "thank God it's Friday" style of thinking about leisure revolves around the habit of "killing time" until the weekend and making the weekend truly memorable. "TGIF" has spawned a series of related credos, like this one overheard in the hall of an office building: "It's Tuesday; we're halfway there!"

A corporate vice president, returning from a professional meeting, captured the "theory" of TGIF. Describing the national board meeting of a professional organization, she said, "They worked hard and they played hard."

The concept of "playing hard" has connotations of sexual and alcoholic excesses, yet for many participants in the TGIF style, playing hard means a deliberate change in activity. For example, Dr. T., a physician, works a 50-hour workweek, but spends every weekend on his sailboat with his wife and two sons. TGIF can also mean planning special getaways, buying tickets to a concert, inviting friends to dinner, or looking forward to love in the afternoon.

Examine your leisure survey: Do you see a pattern of solid work commitments during the week and weekends of wall-to-wall activity? This leisure style can be a positive choice in the sense that participants make definite plans to enjoy time after work. The drawback of the approach is that it tends to overcompensate for the stress and boredom of work and may lead to activities for the sole purpose of escape.

After a difficult week at work, the drive to escape may deprive you of opportunities to engage in stimulating and rewarding activities that can provide rich experiences you don't get on the job.

AGITATE-VEGETATE

The motto of this leisure style can be summed up in an ancient, anonymous proverb: "How wonderful to do nothing and rest afterward."

The agitate-vegitate leisure style has been adapted by millions of workers with high-stress jobs. As you examine your leisure survey you may see a pattern of heated work activity followed by periods of minimal activity or passive entertainment.

"A-V'ers" spend their evenings and weekends sleeping, lounging, watching television, being entertained. Julie M., an industrial psychologist, explains, "I don't want to do a single thing on Saturday except sleep late, listen to relaxing music, and talk to my husband and kids."

It is essential to use time after work for rest and recuperation from job pressures. If you recognize this leisure style, you know that you have learned to relax after work. But don't assume that all other activities will add stress or further deplete your energy reserves. Keep your options open; consider other possibilities for intellectual or physical activity, personal development, or community involvement. You may be delighted and surprised to learn that sleeping and watching video movies are not the only ways to recover from the pressures of your job.

CAMOUFLAGE

The lines at the movie were long and discouraging and Lynn S. and Andy M., both architects, slipped into a nearby bowling alley. The first game was great fun, with both of them scoring in the high eighties. During the second game, Andy got a series of strikes and started to take the game more seriously. Said Lynn, "He stopped laughing when he threw gutter balls and stepped up to the lane with a grim determination.

Once Andy decided to 'get good at it,' I stopped enjoying the game. It had suddenly become work instead of play."

Leisure can easily become a camouflage for the attitudes and habits that we bring home from work. In Andy's case, the concern with attaining a high score replaced his former enjoyment of an unlikely sport.

Although many of us enjoy competitive sports after work, we can draw a distinction between serious business and pleasure. It is important to "play your best" during the handball tournament, but the line is drawn in the enjoyment of the game itself.

Review your leisure survey: Do you see patterns of activity where competition and performance are the focus of your free time? If ever the locker-room motto "it's how you play the game" were appropriate, it's during the hours after work.

Concern with winning is only one of the ways that leisure becomes an extension of work. You may also find that your time after work is spent on activities that closely mirror your on-the-job responsibilities. You may be camouflaging work as play.

LEISURE AS LABOR

You may spend your time after work on "busman's holidays," on work activities thinly disguised as leisure. A busman's holiday has been defined as one where a bus driver takes a dubious vacation by taking his family on a road trip. Other examples: a surgeon carving a Thanksgiving Day turkey, Madonna singing in the shower, Frankenstein working the graveyard shift, and an attorney watching "L.A. Law."

Or you may find that the habits cultivated on the job contribute to unsatisfying leisure time. At the end of a workday or workweek, you may discover that your bedside or deskside manner follows you home after work. Your occupational skills—the way you communicate, make decisions, and manage people on the job—will not be appreciated by friends and family. They will be the first to tell you.

- A teenage daughter to her professor father: "I'm not one of your students, Dad."

- The wife of a political lobbyist to her husband: "You can get off of your soapbox; we are only talking about a movie."

- My husband, Jeremy, to me: "Let's not get so psychoanalytic about it."

Occupational habits can become hazardous to our health when we fail to turn them off after work. Take a closer look at three occupational habits that follow you home and sabotage your effort at self-renewal.

Habit 1: You Are Always "on Call."

A recent study of 500 executives, conducted by Hyatt International, found that while on vacation 70 percent of them said that the office knew where they were at all times, and 30 percent called in constantly. As more companies globalize, you can expect to be pursued at home by calls and faxes from colleagues in other time zones. But sometimes it is our friends and acquaintances who encourage us to work overtime and make "house calls."

One hazard of your job may be that other people expect you to be wearing your professional hat at all times. Physicians, attorneys, psychologists, financial advisors, business owners, and many others can be besieged at social gatherings with questions about their professional expertise. Friends and acquaintances feel free to ask a doctor at half-time of the Super Bowl: "Syd, can you take a look at this mole behind my ear?" Or to ask the stockbroker passing the crudites: "Do you think I should buy IBM now or wait until things stabilize?"

Working professionals need to protect their private time from business inquiries. It is important to warmly, but firmly refuse to talk about business or to render a service on the dance floor.

Giving "free advice" is not the issue; once you start talking about work, you are easily reminded of other problems, other cases you have left behind. You also forfeit the opportunity to allow friends and acquaintances to experience you in another more relaxed role.

TECHNIQUE:
The Assertive Cocktail

You're a lawyer and enjoying a glass of wine and a conversation about the Super Bowl. A casual acquaintance marches up to you and asks, "My sister's husband moved in with his secretary. Does that mean she will automatically get custody of the kids?" You have three choices at that moment.

- You might give an *apologetic* response. Mumbling or shuffling your feet, you'd say: "Uh . . . I'm sorry, I don't handle family law cases."
- Maybe you'll answer with an *aggressive* response. In a loud and tight voice you might ask, "What do you think this is, night court?"
- Your best response would be to change the subject in an *assertive*, friendly manner. Smile and say: "That's a good question, but I'm taking the night off."

Practice saying each of these phrases in three ways: first, *apologetically*, then *aggressively*, then *assertively*.

1. "Sorry, but I left my calculator (stethoscope, slide rule, briefcase) in the office."
2. "That's an interesting problem, but I was hoping to stay out of court (the office, the hospital) this weekend."
3. "You sound concerned; I can talk to you about it on Monday (or tomorrow). Why don't you call me at the office?"
4. "I wish you had asked me that before I had my third glass of champagne. I'll have to take two aspirin and call in the morning."

When you refuse to mix business and pleasure, your friends and acquaintances lose an opportunity for free advice, but gain the chance to engage you in topics unrelated to your work interest.

The idea of protecting your leisure time from work talk is part of the process of learning to use time after work to counterbalance the skills/habits and satisfactions you experience on the job.

Habit 2: You Are Always "on Task."

In a favorite *New Yorker* cartoon of mine, a business-suited man stares out the window at a bird feeder and mutters, "It's been up for two days. If there are no damn birds by tomorrow, down it comes!" This habit of bringing a task/bottom-line orientation home takes two defeating forms: first, the concept of "working around the house," and, second, the need to have tangible results (something to "show for" your time away from work).

Try two tactics to change these nasty habits.

TECHNIQUE:
Lower Your Standards

One of the biggest challenges of leisure time is resisting the executive urge to overschedule your time after work. For example, I often ask a friend what he did over the weekend and he answers, "We raked the leaves, paid bills, cleaned the basement, did ten loads of laundry. . . ." Frequently, a client complains, "I've got an endless 'to do' list in the office, but the one at home is even longer."

I admit that sometimes yardwork and even folding laundry are "grounding rituals"—meditative, relaxing activities. But, in general, I have three words of advice about the agenda list at home: *"Lower your standards."* You simply cannot pursue renewal and domestic perfection at the same time. I invite you either to hire help or to make a choice between the drudgery of bouncing dimes off the bedspread and the delights of self-renewal.

TECHNIQUE:
No Numbers, Please

For those of you who spend your day in the office, glued to the facts and figures of your business life, revitalization lies in changing from a quantitative to a qualitative focus. Like the man with his bird feeder, you need to shift your perspective from the outcome to the experience.

- *Your assignment:* Go to this season's blockbuster movie. And do let yourself laugh, or be scared, or well-up with tears as you are drawn into the characters' foibles and dilemmas. Don't think about how much the movie grossed last week or in how many theaters it's playing.

- *Other Homework:* Do some nonprofessional reading. Do nothing and rest. Make plans that have no redeeming social or economic value.

Habit 3: You Are Always "on Time."

Don Ross, the former CEO of New York Life, leaves his Manhattan office every Friday to go to his country home. On arrival, he takes off his watch, places it on his bureau, and doesn't put it on again until he leaves. His ceremony is symbolic of how a different sense of time contributes to renewal. In this era of shortened development times and delivery schedules, we are always dealing with deadlines. Try these approaches, adapted from Meyer Friedman's suggestions in *Type A Behavior and Your Heart,* to take a vacation from the urgent sense of time in your workplace.

TECHNIQUE:
Time on Your Side

Practice slowing down:

- Drive in the slowest lane on a Sunday afternoon or get in the longest line in the grocery store or toll booth.

- Walk, eat, and talk at a deliberately slower rate. Don't run across the street on a yellow light. Chew each mouthful. Stop finishing a friend's sentences to speed up the conversation.

- Select a time to leave your watch at home. Amuse yourself by counting the times you examine your empty wrist.

A LONG WAY
FROM THE OFFICE

At age 10, I had my first lesson in leisure from my father, a physician who accepted the leading role of Bibinski in the musical *Silk Stockings.* What a demanding role it was; he had to deliver hundreds of lines in a Russian accent, as he sang and danced. I recall my mother, a talented singer, coaching him on his lines and lyrics, but what I remember most is his big production number on opening night.

There we sat, my three sisters and I, unspeakably nervous (when you are 10, your father can really embarrass you). Yet we shouldn't have worried because he was wonderful; he didn't fluff a line, his accent was flawless, his softshoe elegant. After mugging his way through a number called "Hail, Bibinski," he was hoisted atop the shoulders of several burly chorus members and paraded around the stage. I looked at his face—triumphant and half-terrified—and I thought, "Boy, is he a long way from the office!"

My father's stage debut provided a lasting image of the power that life after work has in bringing rewards and stimulation unlike those on the job. Take a moment and think about what might take you a long way from the office.

TECHNIQUE:
School for Play

Let's pause to explore the focus of a classical Greek education. Aristotle, for example, suggested that leisure, rather than work, provided the purest definition of self. But in our society, renewal is not one of the 4 R's taught in the classroom; so let's take this time to look at the balance of satisfactions in your life. Which needs are satisfied at work? After work?

- Physical activity
- Entertainment
- Sensory stimulation
- Personal growth
- Social responsibility
- Creative expression
- Relaxation
- Spirituality
- Self-promotion

- Sense of accomplishment
- Community involvement
- Solitude
- Intellectual challenge
- Spirit of adventure
- Close contact with people
- Recognition
- Opportunity to develop friendships

If your job lacks opportunities in an area of potential satisfaction, have you compensated for this in your time after work? As you think about the counterbalances in your own life, consider several examples.

Accomplishment/Creativity

I'm not suggesting that your time after work be devoted to activity diametrically opposed to work. In fact, many business and professional people enjoy much satisfaction by applying their job skills in radically different settings. *Business Volunteers for the Arts* is a perfect example of this approach. In Boston, San Francisco, and Seattle, business executives volunteer weekly to work with nonprofit arts groups.

Bankers, accountants, and consultants of every description are paired with the artists and boards of directors from opera and ballet companies, new-wave theater groups, or chamber ensembles. The banker who applies his budget skills to become involved in a creative collaboration with a struggling theater group has satisfied needs that go beyond his corporate application of financial skill.

Close Contact/Solitude

The frequency and intensity of your contacts with people at work will influence the balance of social time after work.

Dennis T. spends most of the day alone, feeding numbers into the payroll computer of a large company. He makes a point of scheduling several evenings a week with friends for dinner or a drink.

Jean D. is a psychologist whose days are spent in intense dialogue with her patients. "Everything has *meaning* when you do therapy; nothing is taken for granted. When I come home, I enjoy time alone or lighthearted conversations with my family or friends."

Self-Promotion/Community Involvement

Most professionals and small-business owners spend their workweek in relentless promotion. (See The Darker Side of Networking, Chapter 7.) For them, time after work can be balanced by strong community participation.

Dana K. is the owner of a chain of elegant women's clothing stores. After work, she is deeply involved in the consumer rights movement, attending meetings, planning speakers, raising funds. She feels comfortable balancing promotion of her business with positive contributions to the future of her community.

As you examine the balance between work and leisure in your life, remember you are not alone.

PARTNERS IN PLAY

Whether you live alone or with an extended family, practice thinking of renewal as a joint venture. For those who live solo, the challenge lies in avoiding an empty calendar. Many single, working professionals often make and then cancel plans with friends for the hours after work. Their calendars are overbooked during the day and their evenings and weekends are completely free. Their scheduling points to the strongest advantage and the clearest advantage of coming home alone.

When you first arrive home, you have the opportunity to unwind without meeting the emotional demands of a partner or children. You can enjoy the luxury of a three-hour bubble bath, taking time to cast off your fears about work and to scheme about the future. You can enjoy a leisurely dinner, thinking about the frustrating people in your day and making plans to finish projects tomorrow. The problem arises when your time to unwind extends into the entire evening or weekend.

Without the interruptions of a friend or family member, your pre-occupation with work can continue until you go to sleep. This aspect of living alone can result in constant thoughts about work.

Your empty calendar is the beginning of a life pattern of self-absorption. Each time you decline to join a friend or lover, you reinforce the idea that you cannot manage a life that includes both work and renewal. If your daytime appointments are written in ink, and your evenings with friends in pencil, try two techniques to cultivate the habit of carrying out plans after work.

TECHNIQUE:
Reconnect

Before you reach for the phone to cancel dinner with a friend, think back to the good feelings that prompted you to want to spend time with him or her.

Daniel R., an investment banker, describes the situation: "Some-times at the end of the day I feel too tired or wound up to get together with friends. But, instead of canceling, I let myself remember our last visit. Then I can reconnect with the good feelings I had when we made the plans."

When you can reconnect with positive feelings, your plans for the evening may become appealing. If your imagination doesn't make the connection, pick up the telephone.

TECHNIQUE:
Confirm

In the midst of a busy week, you may approach dinner with a friend as if it were another item on your "agenda" list. If you begin to confuse professional and personal time, call your friend to confirm your dinner together. In many cases, just the sound of your friend's voice will stimulate your memories of good times together and help you to honor your plans to meet. "I can't count the number of times I have called to cancel drinks," said one real estate developer. "But when I call, I hear a friend's voice and suddenly I *want* to get together."

Those of you who live with a partner who resists making renewal a priority, try two approaches to enrich your time together.

TECHNIQUE:
A Little Research

Allison and Peter T. have a delightful division of labor. "Peter is in surgery 10 hours a day. If I didn't find out what was going on in the city, we'd never leave the house." Allison considers it part of her job as a home manager to research possibilities for their leisure time. During the day, she checks out new local restaurants, reads reviews of plays, movies, and concerts, or buys a special bottle of wine. She exchanges information with other mothers about family campsites and programs at local museums.

TECHNIQUE:
Broadening the Circle

You can entice your partner away from problems and personalities on the job by inviting him or her to share your interests in art, politics, athletics, and community. Consider inviting any or all of these people to a casual Sunday barbecue: the woman you met in your French class, a fellow community board member or political campaigner, a couple whose daughter is in your babysitting coop.

Include her in the annual dinner of the volunteer organizations you enjoy. Insist that he join you at the victory celebration of the candidate you supported for mayor. Each occasion offers a refreshing change of scene, an opportunity for you to broaden your interests and circle of friends together, and for your partner, fewer opportunities to think about work or to talk shop.

FOLLOWING THROUGH

You may have grand ideas and strong intentions but you still find yourself canceling plans after work. Let me suggest a series of strategies to help you keep your commitment to rejuvenating leisure time.

TECHNIQUE:
Cancellation Policies

- Buy season tickets to sports events, theater, and concerts, and write the dates on your calendar. Having made the arrangements, you will be less likely to cancel.

- Plan leisure activities with friends. It is easier to cancel your own plans than to break up a doubles tennis match.

- When you volunteer, sign up for specific times and dates.

- When you book ski trips and cabins on the ocean, pay in advance. Preregister for classes and lecture series. Your financial investment may prevent you from canceling.

- Announce your intentions to other people. Having talked about your trip to the Caribbean for weeks, you don't want to explain to 35 people why you don't have a tan.

Pause for a moment now, and list 10 activities that bring meaning and delight to your life after work. Next to each activity, note the last time you enjoyed the refreshing activity. Has it been weeks? Months? Years?

I know you are faced with an avalanche of work—a new boss or staff member, project deadline or quota concerns, presentation or new information system—and you just don't have time for fishing, or learning French, or attending the opera, or volunteering for United Way. Besides, in a ferociously competitive marketplace, all of that is frivolous.

May I remind you that even samurai warriors retreated from the battlefield? In their retreat, they meditated, painted, and wrote poetry—activities that took them a long way from their work on the battlefield.

PART FOUR

Parents' Rules
of Renewal

9

Unwinding:
For Parents and Kids

"*It's* a beautiful day in the neighborhood, a beautiful day for a neighbor," sings the loopy Mr. Rogers as he turns in his suit and puts on a Jello-colored sweater at the beginning of the most parodied children's show in television history. Responses to "Mr. Roger's Neighborhood" run the gamut: from Eddie Murphy's streetwise sendup on "Saturday Night Live" to writer Anna Quindlan's claim that the theme song has been linked to an outbreak of parental hives. I prefer the response of Kevin C., a financial executive, who tapes the show on his VCR and sits down to watch it with his three-year-old son as a way of making the end-of-the-day transition together.

As a parent, you could measure the end of the day in units of transitions per minute. You must adjust to leaving your workplace and greeting your partner and children. As a single parent, without the buffer of the extra heart and hands of a partner, the transition from the "to do" list on the job to the one at home can be daunting prospect.

Dan P., an accountant, describes the end of his day: "First I pick up Cyndy at her office, then we drive to the day-care center to collect our daughter. As we drive home, we are like three people coming home from work; all of us wanting to process our day at the same time."

While you are at work, your children are experiencing a series of stresses and triumphs that parallel the events of your day. When you greet your children, the success of your evening will depend, in part, on how each of you has dealt with the day's problems.

This chapter underlines the importance of transitional techniques for working parents, reviews the pressures of a child's "day at school," and suggests quick and efficient techniques for parents who have little time to unwind.

Let's begin with the babysitter's report and with the stresses lurking in the classroom and on the playground.

WHAT THE BABYSITTER SAW

As the parent of an infant or preschool-age child, you will be greeted by a babysitter or a day-care worker at the end of the day. At the same time you are reviewing your day, the babysitter is providing you with the highlights of your child's day. Important areas of review include how the young child ate and slept, which toys he enjoyed, and how he responded to the sitter, teacher, and other children.

Janet R., a banker, describes picking up her eight-week-old baby at an infant development center. "At the end of the day, they'd tell us about her mood, her responsiveness, and her eye movements. But my husband and I were so exhausted, all I remember about those first six months of being back at work is coming home and lying down on the couch. My main topic of conversation with Ken was 'Are we more tired than we are hungry?'"

School-age children will tell you very directly about their day and may expect your full attention.

HOW CHILDREN COME HOME FROM SCHOOL

"When I pick up my daughter," one father reported, "I am suddenly thrust into the world of children." Within that world, each of the problems outlined in the first chapter may also concern your school-age child. Children have their own version of a fast pace, unfinished symphonies, and encounters with difficult people. They come home with unexpressed feelings about these people and pressures, feelings that may greet you and demand to be heard as you walk through the front door.

Here is a child-sized inventory of the stresses of the day.

The Fast Lane

During a typical school day, younger children cover basic subject matter in swift, hourly chunks. By lunch time, your son may have tackled problems in long division, completed a watercolor drawing, taken a spelling test, and learned that George Washington had false teeth.

In high school, your daughter is solving for x one hour and conjugating a verb in French an hour later. She steps off the volleyball court and walks into her economics class. Tonight, she may be able to explain deficit spending.

After the age of seven or eight, most school-age children rapidly shift gears to a series of after-school activities as diverse as Cub Scouts, Junior Achievement, music lessons, drama club, or just "hanging out" with friends. A therapist, and the mother of a nine-year-old, commented: "Jonathan's schedule is beginning to look like mine!" And the parents of teenagers will soon be pleading to be kept informed about the social calendars of their children. "We have reached the 'where are you going?' stage," lamented one parent.

This rapid pace leaves many young people tired at the end of the day and the numerous activities create many possibilities to carry home unfinished business.

Unfinished Symphonies

The youthful version of unfinished business usually takes the form of homework: a math test, a science project, or three chapters of *The Scarlet Letter* to be read by tomorrow. Other unfinished business involves a series of logistical problems that require your attention. These can include a note for the school field trip, clay for an art project, your signature on a driver's permit form, and cookies for a school open house.

Social agendas are another source of concern. There are parties to be planned, friends invited to spend the night, dates accepted and rejected, and phone calls to return. Along with their social calendar, kids of all ages come home with strong feelings about the people in their day.

Uninvited Guests

Often, your children will literally "bring a friend home." On other occasions, much to your dismay, your first hour at home will be spent listening to a blow-by-blow description of your son's teacher.

Depending on the age of your children, the following uninvited guests may become regulars at your dinner table.

- The kids on the bus: "David said I was fat. I'm not fat, am I?"

- Fair-weather friends: "I don't trust her anymore; she told Alice everything I said."

- Young love: "I don't trust her anymore; she told everything I said."

Unexpressed Feelings

Your child's feelings about important people and unfinished business may be very strong, but the feelings may be camouflaged and unspoken. They may be communicated to you in code.

Linda G., an accountant, is familiar with veiled messages. "I can always tell when my teenage son is upset; he'll pick a fight and go back 100 years. He will say: 'Remember that time you wouldn't let me go to the Michael Jackson concert?' If we continue talking, and I can keep my temper, I will usually find out that something at school or a conflict with a friend is the real source of the problem."

But keeping your temper while your children "unwind from school" can be a Herculean task.

UNWINDING WITH YOU
AND WITHOUT YOU

School-age kids have opportunities to unwind before they see you. Your children may take the bus, walk, or ride a bike home from school. Often accompanied by their friends, they trade gossip and secrets; they swap homework and assurances. They debrief the day among friends.

Many kids play physical games after school: bicycling, soccer, Frisbee, and football. Kids of all ages watch TV and create snacks of every possible description.

Younger children seem to want company after school and teenagers seem to cherish time alone. Sharon, 13, described her homecoming rituals. "When I am walking home, I feel tired. I walk in the door and fix myself a cup of tea. I turn on the TV and stare at it; I'm not really watching it, but I'm trying not to think about my day."

For most kids, the ritual of unwinding after school is not complete until you come home or pick them up at school or the babysitter. Nancy, an interior designer, asked her son Daniel, 12, and her daughter Miriam, 9, "What is the first thing you want when I walk through the front door?" "I want attention," said Miriam. "I want you to hug me and let me tell you about school." "Not me," said Daniel. "I want to know what's for dinner."

These needs are typical of the situations that face you when you walk through the front door, after work. Your children want your warm greetings and an opportunity to gain your ear. They may also make immediate demands about domestic responsibilities, like laundry and dinner.

Most parents look forward to seeing their children at the end of the day. Greg N., a management consultant, describes his daughter as *the* reason to work hard at making the transition after work." And parents enjoy the process of "show and tell." The problem is that the "show" often begins the moment they walk through the door, before they have had time to unwind from the pressures of work.

If you hope to respond warmly to the immediate needs of your family, it is absolutely essential that you give yourself a chance to unwind before coming home. But time is a precious commodity to working parents. You'll need quick and efficient techniques to accomplish the transition from harried professional to loving parent.

UNWINDING AT
100 MILES PER HOUR

A working mother, attending one of my workshops about coming home, said in exasperation, "These techniques for transition are straight from Fantasyland. I don't have *time* to unwind before I see my kids!"

She was right about the time shortage. Parents need to unwind and adjust to coming home more quickly than other working people. But she was mistaken to think that she could head straight home. Every working person needs to incorporate rituals that acknowledge the end of the day and the beginning of an evening at home. Parents who skip this step put their families at risk.

Diana M., an insurance executive and a single parent, isn't willing to take the risk. "I need time to walk away from my work situation. Sometimes I'll pay the sitter an extra $5 so I can go to the gym. The damage I do in the first 5 minutes can ruin the evening with my son. If I exercise, I feel that when I come home, I'm there to stay."

Parents, and especially single parents, don't have time after work for a two-hour bubble bath with Nancy Reagan (see Chapter 1). But every parent should allot at least a small amount of time to disengage from the pressures of work.

Limited time means that as parents, you will have to be creative and nimble in accomplishing your transitional rituals; it doesn't mean that you skip them. You may need to combine techniques for unwinding with some of the responsibilities of family life.

There is no question that you will be moving at a speed of 100 miles per hour. Why not practice some of the techniques while grocery shopping or picking up your daughter from softball practice?

Let's reexamine the five problems of homecoming (slowing down, unfinished business, unexpressed feelings, loss of humor, and self-absorption) and consider the most time-efficient techniques to reduce the problems.

Problem: Slowing Down

In Chapter 1, I suggested that you might slow down by saving the easiest tasks of the day for last (see Technique: Slowing Down). I also suggested a 5-minute trip to Tahiti (see Technique: Postcards from Tahiti). If you don't feel comfortable sitting still for 5 minutes, or you have trouble visualizing, try an alternative vacation.

TECHNIQUE:
Four Fast Vacations

As you drive home or ride the bus or train, you can use a series of sounds to transport yourself to a more restful location. Mike Kron, an acoustician at New York–based Syntonic Research, describes a number of albums and cassettes called "Environments" that can be purchased at local record stores.

Choose among four fast vacations: sailing, a walk on the beach, an English meadow at dawn, or a thunderstorm atop a Manhattan apartment. Tape addicts have reported that they use the tapes on headsets and in cars on their way home. Others listen when they come home. One happy listener reported, "These tapes have replaced my martini."

But you may be thinking, "I can't listen to the tapes; I have to pick up my kids on my way home."

TECHNIQUE:
Four Fast Family Vacations

You can plan to include other family members on your brief vacations. If you play the tapes in the car, explain to your kids that the sounds help you to relax, to feel good.

Don't be surprised if your children become absorbed in the sounds. Mike Kron explains, "The strongest application of the environmental tapes has been to help students of all ages study. They are a means of stimulating imagination that have been used by teachers all over the country."

Even if the family doesn't listen in silence, the background can have a soothing effect on the conversation and on you. "In some cases," reports Kron, "the tapes can become associated with a particular activity. Think of the possibilities: Your family might think of the ride home as a walk through the meadow or a jaunt on a sailboat."

Even on a sailboat, you may have been thinking about the work problems that pursue you.

Problem: Postponing Unfinished Business

With so little time to unwind, you may want to delegate tasks to the resources of your unconscious mind (see Technique: Delegate to Your Unconscious Mind, Chapter 1). The application of *thought stopping* (see Technique: Thought Stopping, Chapter 1) will also help postpone thoughts about your unfinished business.

For another speedy means of closure, practice a technique perfected by a working parent.

TECHNIQUE:
"Goodbye, Office"

Jean S., a warm and witty therapist, describes her special technique of postponing office business. "I decided to get more formal about saying goodbye at the end of the day. I used to casually say to my secretary and associates, 'So long; see you tomorrow.' Now I make a point of finding each one and saying goodbye more formally. I walk outside of my office, close the door, and say, *goodbye* office."

She continues, "Just as important, when I see my son, I make a special effort to give him more than a casual greeting. I make a big point of saying hello with a hug and a kiss. I put into words how glad I am to see him."

Practice mentally closing the doors to your office and saying "goodbye, office" on your way home to your family. This technique takes less than a minute and provides a definite recognition of the end of the day.

Problem: Feelings About Difficult People

As you end the day, make time for a brief, emotional conference with yourself. This can be accomplished by rolling the credits (see Technique: Roll the Credits, Chapter 1) and connecting with your feelings about the important people in your day.

Strong feelings about work often have "no place to go." How about putting them in a plain brown wrapper?

TECHNIQUE:
The Boss's Brown Paper Bag

Sharon F., a market researcher, likes to keep a brown paper bag on the front seat of her car. Her previous boss suggested this technique. "He said that before coming to work, he would place the bag over his mouth and talk about each of his concerns. He'd try to talk about his wife and kids and then leave his feelings *in the bag* so that he could concentrate on work."

After work, you can collect all of your feelings about difficult people in the same paper bag and leave it on the front seat of the car. This silly and symbolic act may help you to regain your sense of humor.

Problem: Loss of Humor

Facing your family without a sense of humor can be a dangerous mission. Yet, the day may leave you drained, without a giggle in sight. The fastest technique for finding humor can involve a game with one of your children.

TECHNIQUE:
The Funniest Thing

Joel Goodman, father and editor of the journal *Laughing Matters,* describes a game that a parent and child can play. It is a game that requires a sense of humor. The rules are simple. Each working day, both parent and child share a ritual dialogue. Each person takes a turn, telling/asking "What is the funniest or nuttiest thing that happened to you today?"

As you leave work, review your day for comic material. Using the hints in Chapter 1, select one event and transform it into a funny story. Knowing that your child expects to hear a comic tale can help revive your battered sense of humor. Exchanging funny stories is a way of easing the transition and developing the habit of good humor in your family.

Problem: Self-Absorption

Everyone who spends the day concentrating on work will be focused on his or her own thoughts at the end of the day. Try managing the problem of self-absorption with the technique of headlining (Chapter 3). Then use the technique of glimpsing (Chapter 3) to create a mental picture of family members waiting for you at home.

Some parents prefer to preview their evenings at home with a phone call.

TECHNIQUE:
Previewing

Many working parents ask their children to call them at work when they get home. Whether your child is home alone or with a babysitter, a telephone preview can help prevent you from being overwhelmed by a barrage of stories and demands when you walk through the door.

Listening to your child talk briefly about the day gives you a preview of emotional needs and logistical demands. You can learn, for example, that your son was disappointed because he didn't get selected for the school play or that your daughter needs special glue for her science project.

Sometimes a parent can miss crucial information on a previewing phone call. Gina D., a mother of two, reported a phone call in which her older son had "some good news and some bad news." "Of course, I told him: 'Tell me the good news first.' We talked about three minutes about how pleased he was about his score on a math test. Then I said, 'What's the bad news?' 'The bad news is about Jimmy,' he said quickly. 'Two kids are beating him up outside!'"

When you give yourself time to confront the five problems of homecoming, you can arrive with some semblance of sanity. If you walk through the door with a briefcase full of feelings, you may spend the rest of the evening undoing the effect of your entrance.

10

Homecoming Habits

*E*very evening, single parent Yvonne B., an information services executive, walks through the front door and hugs each of her three children, who chorus, "Mom, do you have any homework tonight?" With this delightful homecoming habit, Yvonne's family paves the way for a smooth transition. Yet when you confront the immediate emotional and logistical demands of your family, you may be unable to instantly respond with affection. Instead, you may remind your children of two characters from the pages of their storybooks.

THE QUEEN OF HEARTS

Alice had been in Wonderland for only a short time when she learned that the Queen of Hearts was something less than an enlightened despot. The Queen had absolutely no tolerance for frustration or conflict. At the first sign of a problem, she would issue her famous, brittle command: "Off with his head!"

Weary with the demands of reigning her kingdom, she felt justified in her self-indulgent commands and capricious punishments. In a similar way, for many exhausted parents, particularly those who are greeted by fighting siblings, the threshold of the door can quickly become a scaffold.

Norma S., a designer, admits to past moments of self-indulgence: "If I had a hard day, I'd either walk through the door and blow up or run upstairs and take a shower, whichever I got to first! In the past couple of years, I have learned to discipline myself, to go through my kids' rituals first, to meet their needs first, and *then* to go upstairs and change my clothes and wash my face."

Exercising self-control when you walk through the front door takes a strong, concerted effort. Your kids may want the most attention from you at the moment when you have the least to give.

Some days you will feel like you are about to metamorphose into the Queen of Hearts. Before you start to order beheadings, or the parental equivalent of grounding, why not hold court for a few minutes?

TECHNIQUE:
Holding Court

"Holding court" when you come home from work means that for the first 10 or 15 minutes, you concentrate all of your attention on your children and then excuse yourself for some royal recuperation. One couple even sets a kitchen timer for 15 minutes; they escape upstairs and return when the timer buzzes.

Monica H., a real estate broker, describes the technique: "Sandra has been home for a couple of hours alone by the time I get home. She sees me and she wants to spell out everything! She wants to talk about homework, and her girlfriends and boyfriend and plans for the weekend. I listen to her for a couple of minutes, and *then* I say hello to George and take off my coat!"

Holding court can protect your homecoming from catastrophe. For a brief period, focus on the immediate needs of your children. Then excuse yourself, without guilt, for a moment of silence. But maybe you are already feeling guilty when you make your entrance.

HANSEL AND GRETEL'S FATHER

Hansel and Gretel's father was feeling guilty and who could blame him? He worked as a woodcutter, barely eking out a living, and on the day in question, he allowed his new wife to talk him into abandoning his children in the forest.

The children's stepmother outlined the plan: "Tomorrow we will take the children to the heart of the forest and give them each a piece of bread; then we will go back to our work and they will never be able to find their way back home." This guilty father did not enjoy a single joyous moment until Hansel and Gretel, through a series of storybook coincidences, returned home.

Hansel and Gretel's father was a parent who felt overcome by remorse and with good reason. Yet so many parents sour their own homecoming with crippling feelings of guilt that are *not* based in reality. Working mothers, in particular, can come home feeling and acting as if they have "abandoned their children in the forest." Guilt feelings keep these parents from taking time to practice techniques for unwinding, and propel them into spending every minute of the evening with their children.

Tanya L., a marketing specialist, explains: "When I come home, I want to spend a little time alone. But I feel guilty; I feel I owe my daughter the time. I think that if I were a better parent, I'd be more available to her at the end of the day."

Many working parents experience guilt feelings about not "being a good enough parent." Other parents feel guilty because their thoughts about their children are not totally positive, or because of resentful feelings about how children infringe on their leisure time or time together as partners.

Guilt feelings are based on an equation between what is ideal behavior and our actual behavior. If the gap between your ideal expectations and your everyday behavior is too great, you can be overwhelmed by guilt.

Guilt is a sad substitute for the delights and frustrations of family life; it is a distracting emotion. You can reduce the distraction by exploring the source of your ideal expectations and verbalizing them.

TECHNIQUE:
Consider the Source

Every family has a set of unwritten ideals about family life. Think back to your family of origin and list some of the attitudes and expectations about "being a family" that were conveyed to you by your own parents and extended family. Try to recall your own ideals as you grew toward parenthood.

You can stimulate your memory by asking these questions. In your family, what were your mother's primary responsibilities? Your father's? Did your parents act as if their relationship or "the kids" came first? When you were growing up, who seemed like a great parent to you? Why? What was on your list of things that you promised you would *never* do when you were a parent? What was on the list of things you promised *always* to remember when you were a parent? Now, review the list and answer the questions from your present point of view. Note the difference and discuss them with your spouse or a close friend.

Your past is not the only source of the ideals and expectations that you use for inducing guilt. Consider any of your peers who you view as "ideal parents" or movies, TV shows, or books that excite you about the possibilities of parenting. Take an honest look at the real and legendary parental ideals you are carrying as you make your entrance after work. These ideals may be keeping you from enjoying your strengths and limitations as a parent. Instead of coming home like a "guilty character," learn to recognize the source of your unrealistic expectations and to treat your best attempts with humor and generosity.

Brad D., a single parent and physician, captures the essence of this self-acceptance as a parent. "Sometimes I think I ought to be giving her more time. But damn it, I'm tired and sometimes I give her some things she can play with on her own. I mean, I can only play *Chutes and Ladders* so many times!"

Another father who delights in seeing his daughter warmly acknowledges the loss of his own leisure time and time alone with his wife. He laughs and warns, "Don't ever let *anyone* tell you that having kids won't change your relationship!"

Families can develop a repertoire of good habits, supported by the idea of realistic expectations for both parents and children. Such habits will prevent guilty and self-indulgent characters from making an entrance.

GOOD HABITS START EARLY

I saw a charming commercial directed to parents. The ad shows a grade-school class on a field trip. The teacher does a quick head count and discovers that one of the children is missing. A frantic search uncovers her whereabouts; she is in the bathroom brushing her teeth. The commentary: "Good habits start early."

The tone of your family life and your children's habits are guided by the behavior you model and the suggestions and expectations you communicate from their earliest years. Consider seven good habits that can add grace and joy to your family's transition after work and school.

Good Habit 1: Encourage Activities That Help Family Members to Unwind

This habit can begin by your example. Let your children know at an early age that you are involved in various activities that help you unwind after work. Even a four-year-old can understand these explanations:

- "Come talk to me while I jump (on the trampoline) or ride the bike. I am really tired today; I think riding will help me wake up."

- "I'm going to run upstairs and change my clothes. I love to put on a sweatshirt—like the one you have—when I get home."

  The idea of unwinding might be inaugurated by a simple conversation.

  Parent: Do you ever feel tired after school?

  Child: Sometimes.

  Parent: What do you do when you feel tired?

  Child: I don't know, maybe take a nap or watch TV.

Parent: Sometimes I feel tired when I get home, too. Taking a run really gives me energy. When I feel refreshed, we can have more fun together after dinner.

Modeling the fact that you need to unwind is an ideal way to introduce the idea of transition to your family. You can also encourage your kids to structure their own time after school to meet some of their own needs. Here are some possibilities:

- Show an interest in activities besides school and school work. Don't just ask "What did you do in school?" Also ask "What did you do *after* school?"

- Don't insist that homework be done before dinner. Suggest that the work needs to be done by 8 o'clock and let your child decide whether she wants to get it out of the way or to "hang out" and do it after dinner.

- Encourage activities that help kids unwind. Let them spend time on the phone to friends (within limits) or time visiting friends. Stock nutritious snacks, like fruit, vegetable sticks, and wholesome cookies.

- Encourage children to exercise after school through bike rides with friends, school sports, and walks with you. Remember that the "fight-or-flight" impulse is alive in children, too; they too accumulate tensions throughout the day.

- Expose them to the possibilities of after-school interests (besides TV) that will help them relax. Browse with your child in a hobby store and see if anything catches her or his eye. Encourage your son or daughter to collect anything that interests them, including stamps, bottles, coins, and rock star autographs. Visit bookstores and let each child buy the book of his or her choice. Let each choose a magazine; then sign them up for a subscription and let them watch for it in the mail. Take your kids to the ballet, symphony, popular concerts (until they won't be seen with you), and jazz performances. Allow for the possibility of dance or music lessons. Buy them an inexpensive stereo or tape deck and let them listen to their choice of music. You might also invest in earphones.

Good Habit 2:   Encourage Your Family to Put Their Feelings into Words

The good habit of talking about feelings begins with your own example. Anna B., a corporate attorney, believes that her own openness encourages her children to talk about school. "I try not to just pry. So, I try to say something about my day, too. I can be honest; I can admit I had a crummy day. When I open up to my son, he seems to open up to me, too. He'll tell me about something that is bothering him and I'll commiserate and say, 'It sounds like a bad day for both of us; the stars must have been in the wrong place!'"

It is important to set limits about how much you disclose to your children. Editing is important in these conversations. Anna can't expect her son to understand the labyrinth of corporate politics, but she can identify some basic feelings about her day. Her son will understand his mother's essential, unspoken message: "I am willing to talk."

If your son or daughter doesn't volunteer information, you can try to ask questions. This maneuver is delicate, because you don't want to nag or pry. Be prepared to ask several questions and then retreat and allow your child some privacy.

The best questions are "essay questions" followed by *paraphrasing*, rather than *advice*.

TECHNIQUE:
Closed Questions, Multiple Choice, Essays

School-age children can easily recognize the difference between a closed question, an essay question, and multiple-choice questions. Closed and multiple-choice questions take only a second to answer and don't allow for an expansive response. An essay question allows for a more detailed, richer answer.

Your questions about your child's day need to be gentle, interested probes; they are not a test. Be careful or the questioning process may remind your kids of a "pop quiz."

Closed Question

Parent: (Noticing that son is particularly quiet) Did you have a bad day today?

Son: No.

End of conversation. If your goal is to allow for a discussion of feelings, try not to ask a question that can be answered with a yes or no. You'd want a yes or no answer if you asked whether the meat loaf was in the oven.

Multiple Choice

Parent: You seem quiet. Are you tired, are you upset with David, or did that math test wipe you out?

Daughter: I am just tired.

End of conversation. Try not to ask multiple-choice questions. Kids will choose one of the choices and the potential for shared feelings may be lost.

Essay Question

Parent: You seem quiet. Something about school wasn't the greatest?

Daughter: You can say that again. Debbie decided to work with someone else on our science project.

Essay questions allow for your son or daughter to describe a difficult or exciting situation. This initial description will give you the opportunity to look for feelings that you can paraphrase.

Review the art of paraphrasing in Chapter 5. After your child has answered an essay question, you'll be able to paraphrase the feelings and situation so that the conversation can continue.

Daughter: You can say that again. Debbie decided to work with someone else on our science project.

Parent: You were really counting on her and she let you down.

Daughter: I thought she was my friend; I don't see how she could change her mind like that.

This conversation has a future. Learn to ask open-ended questions that can be followed by a restatement of the strong feelings your child expresses.

Also learn to be comfortable with silence. Sometimes even the most eloquent essay questions fail to elicit a response. When this happens, smile warmly and say, "I can see that you don't feel like talking right now. Let me know if you change your mind."

Good Habit 3: Encourage Family Members to Understand Each Other's Point of View

Family members adjust more easily to changes and transitions when they can empathize or see the world through each other's eyes. Empathy is grounded in the capacity to picture another person's situation. The art of paraphrasing is an empathic skill, but younger children cannot be expected to paraphrase feelings. Still, the capacity to understand others is a habit that can be acquired early with family field trips and games.

TECHNIQUE:
Field Trips

You can bring children of all ages on a field trip to your office. Show them your desk and some of your products, projects, or work in progress; have them meet your secretary or coworkers. If you don't feel comfortable introducing your family into your professional setting, bring the kids in on Saturday. The ability to picture you at work is a first step in the development of empathy.

Carla N. is an account executive whose family has developed a dinner-hour game to learn to take each other's perspective.

TECHNIQUE:
Trading Places

In this game, family members sit in each other's "usual" place at the dinner table. Next, they take on the role of the person who usually sits in the chair.

Carla explains, "Tim sits in my chair and imitates me talking about my day. I sit in his chair; I imitate his table manners and talk about his teachers. The game leads to lots of laughter and denial: 'I don't do that, do I?'"

Carla's family is happily involved in the process of developing the habit of empathy. Observing and imitating other family members can be a first step in learning to understand the world from their perspective.

Good Habit 4: Encourage Each Person to Contribute to Family Life

My sister Cora describes a wonderful dinner party hosted by our niece and nephew, Hilary, age 8, and Adam, age 10. The menu was falafel, salad, sweet rolls, macaroni, and a castle cake covered with gum drops. Their mother provided baked chicken. "No wine was served because the special beverage was a drink concocted from milk, orange sherbet, and 7-Up. Adam kept asking me, 'Can I get you a refill?' The best part of the dinner was that the kids were so proud of themselves."

You can encourage the habit of making a contribution when your kids come home from school. Too many homecomings are marred by the crush to take care of logistics, like making dinner and doing the wash. Kids feel proud of their involvement at home, and when you take care of domestic chores together, you allow for more creative and playful time.

Lucia D., a college administrator, reported, "When my kids were two and three years old, they started to help to get dinner ready. They would set the table, cut up the fruit, and spill the juice all over the floor . . . . But they felt important, involved. I heard them tell their friends that they helped at home. And we had more time together for talks and for stories."

The key to developing the habit of contributing is to have reasonable expectations and to lower your own standards. The kids may add too much soap to the wash or leave spots on the glasses; they may put the fork on the wrong side of the plate.

Follow some guidelines for encouraging their contributions.

- Don't expect them to do things the way you would. If they tear up the lettuce for a salad, don't complain if you get a piece the size of a palm branch.

- Choose tasks that are age appropriate. A four-year-old can wash tomatoes for a salad. A ten-year-old can empty the dishwasher.

- Don't overload them so that they don't have time to unwind from school. Always praise them for their contribution. Help them understand that cooperation can lead to more relaxed time with you.

Don't expect too much. They are, after all, just kids. Adam, the orange drink host, reminded his mother of this fact when she asked him to make the quiche recipe he had learned at school. He refused, saying "I want to play on the playground, for God sakes!"

Good Habit 5: Learn to Develop a Sense of Timing

Time management is an adult concept, the subject of thousands of words in print and a centerpiece of corporate training. But the ability to use a sense of timing doesn't begin on your first job. It is a habit that can be developed early.

If your children can develop some sense of timing, you can ease the transition between work and home. You'll be able to cut down on the number of urgent logistical requests that eat up your evenings and reduce the family's leisure time on the weekends.

You can encourage a sense of timing in these ways:

- Teach your kids to anticipate their needs for money and errands whenever possible. You can expect them to keep an eye on library book due dates or on a lunch ticket with two more punches. Ask them to list anticipated needs on a family "to do" list.

- Discourage the concept of "This will only take a minute." Help teach your kids to estimate how much time a task, errand, or playful pasttime will occupy. Explain, for example, that they can't shop for shoes, get help on a science project, and go to a matinee on Saturday from 1 o'clock to 3 o'clock. Estimate time out loud for them: "Let's see, the shoes will probably take 30 minutes and the movie is 2 hours long."

- Encourage them to think about their priorities or what is most important. If you can't accomplish everything on Saturday, ask "What is the most important?" Let them answer: "The shoes, I guess. I need them on Monday. Maybe we could work on my project tomorrow."

- You can teach them about the idea of scheduling and post a family calendar in the kitchen. Hold regular family conferences to juggle schedules. Help them learn to respect your time, too. You are available to them, but you may need advance notice. One father and mother require at least a 24-hour warning to attend a PTA meeting.

Kids need to know that you are responsive to their needs, but that you also need time to take care of your own needs. In particular, you need time to spend alone and with your partner or friends.

Good Habit 6:   Encourage the Recognition of Private Time

It was probably inevitable: a set of greeting cards for working parents. One card shows a suited woman coming home with the message, "Every working mother is entitled to some time alone." Open the card and see her surrounded by three kids, a dog, and a cat, each demanding her immediate attention. The card reads, *"Time's up."*

Even when your children are young, you can begin to model the idea that time alone is an important part of family life. Many a homecoming is ruined by the prospect of partners who have no time alone or time together. Many parents feel guilty about wanting to be alone with their spouse. It is important to remember that a strong marriage, nurtured by rich communication and sexual expression, is the foundation of a happy family.

You can express the value of private time in a number of ways:

- Respect your children's need for private time. This need will be strongest beginning in the preteen years. One father explains, "When I come home I make a point of hugging her and saying hello, but I leave her alone in her room until she is ready to talk to me."

- Make a date with each child for some private one-to-one time. Taking your daughter to lunch or to a movie can help her to understand the private time you spend with your friends and partner.

- Communicate the strong value of private time. If you trade off private time with your partner, let your children know that Mom's evening with her friends is special and important.

- Try to introduce your desire for time alone with affection. It is important that your children grow with the understanding that your time spent alone is not a punishment; it is a special and essential time for you.

- Learn to feel comfortable closing your doors after 9 o'clock and allowing for sweet time with your partner. Explain warmly: "Mom and Dad need time to talk and to feel close to each other."

Good Habit 7: Encourage Your Family Members to Talk About Topics Other than Work and School

Among my dearest memories of growing up are the discussions that enlivened my family's dinner table. This tradition began as a part of a Friday night Sabbath meal. Everything about that night was special, even our dress. My three sisters and I wore skirts instead of jeans to the table; we sat in the dining room and my mother would create one of her memorable dinners.

Most discussions began with one of my parents asking each of us to take a turn answering a specific question: "Do you think the death penalty is wrong?" "Does God exist?" "Should women be drafted?"

In these discussions, we learned to talk about a world larger than our classrooms and to verbalize our thoughts and feelings. I remember going to other kids' houses for dinner and being surprised that they didn't talk around the table. *Good habits start early.*

Family discussions can be encouraged in a number of ways.

- With younger kids, read a short story or a riddle that evokes feelings and opinions. Sid Simon's quizzical, provocative stories in his book *Values Clarification* are a good source. So is Gregory Stock's *Kids' Book of Questions.*

- Use topics of school papers as a springboard to other topics, for example, pollution problems, suggested by a science paper.

- Initiate discussions about various aspects of family life. You might say, "I read a study in the paper today that said kids over the age of 10 don't like to stay with babysitters. If you were a parent, how would you decide when to leave kids at home alone?"

- Bring in a clipping from the newspaper, preferably *not* one about how smoking marijuana leads to permanent hair loss, and ask for each person's opinion.

- Read the sports page and follow local teams. Learn the language of sports and how to predict the winner of this year's Super Bowl.

- Initiate political conversations. Older kids can form opinions about candidates. Younger ones can answer "political" questions: "If you were elected President, what would be the first thing you would do?"

- Discuss possibilities for family vacations or weekend activities. Bring travel brochures or announcements of special events and let family members express their preferences for your time together.

The success of these discussions depends on your willingness to listen to the thoughts and feelings of family members. You need to share the floor and allow for opinions very different from your own. Give each person a chance to speak without interruption. Let younger kids speak first. If the age disparity is too great, let the older kids moderate the discussion or interview their younger brothers or sisters.

Allow room for opinions that don't suit yours: kids can smell a brainwashing session from miles away. Try to paraphrase each child's viewpoint rather than press your own.

You can start these discussions at any time in the life of your family. Listening to your children's ideas can become a most delightful way of coming to understand each child's special personality. Richard G., an engineer, talks about the joy of talking and listening to his daughter. "When I get home, I can hang out with Sherry and see what's coming up for her. I can discover what she has learned that day and share her excitement, because everything is new."

Listening to your children can help to ease your homecoming, and the enjoyment of your family can be one of the most scenic routes to self-renewal.

The Business of
Self-Renewal

At a pink-roofed Bermuda resort—where top sales performers were celebrating their success—beach party host and Lotus Development's CEO, Jim Manzi, talked to me about balance and business. "I have some very strict rules for myself: When I am in town, I come into the office very early so I can leave at a reasonable hour and I try hard not to work on the weekends. *Of course, I don't know if I would want my employees to follow this plan,*" he joked, knowing that tomorrow his "state of the union" address would be followed by my seminar on self-renewal.

By now you know that self-renewal is serious business, an essential survival strategy to energize your performance under pressure. You know, too, how self-renewal can enrich both business and pleasure. As you have read these pages, I trust that I have been able to wear down your resistance to renewal.

Instead of "giving at the office" and promising loved ones that your absence is "temporary," you can now shape rituals of transition that protect your private life as a haven for recovery from career demands. Rather than riding an uninterrupted horizon of work and viewing balance as a well-intentioned fantasy, you now understand that self-renewal is, in itself, a professional tool to revive energy, restore perspective, stamina, and creativity, and enhance strategic decision making.

As the business climate grows hotter, expect to be surprised when your organization offers support and innovative ideas as well as executive role models that recognize how balance is good for business. Here's a final and favorite example.

At an "Ask the CEO" session of Sundor Brands, a beverage company that was acquiring an average of two companies a year, one bold employee had the temerity to ask CEO Jim Pomroy, "Where do you see yourself in two years?" Pomroy, a good-humored golfer, waited a dramatically long time to answer. When he did, he put the full weight of his authority behind the art of self-renewal: "In two years? I see myself shooting in the low seventies."